OMNIVM LVX CIVIVM

BOSTON PUBLIC LIBRARY

D1064977

Alpines in colour

Alpines in colour

Will Ingwersen

BLANDFORD

Blandford

an imprint of
Cassell plc
Villiers House, 41/47 Strand
London WC2N 5JE

First published 1981
as *Alpine Garden Plants*
This edition, revised, 1991

British Library Cataloguing in Publication Data
Ingwersen, Will *1905–1990*
    Alpines in colour – 2nd ed.
    1. Gardens. Rock plants. Alpine plants
    I. Title   II. Townsend, Harry *1936–* III. Ingwersen, Will
    1905–1990. Alpine garden plants
    635.952

ISBN 0–7137–2281–9

Distributed in the United States by
Sterling Publishing Co., Inc.,
387 Park Avenue South, New York, NY 10016–8810

Distributed in Australia by
Capricorn Link (Australia) Pty Ltd
PO Box 665, Lane Cove, NSW 2066

Printed and bound in Hong Kong by
South China Printing Co. (1988) Ltd.

Contents

Metric Conversion Table

Length (approx)

$\frac{1}{2}$ in = 1.25 cm	7 in = 17.75 cm
1 in = 2.5 cm	8 in = 20.5 cm
2 in = 5.0 cm	9 in = 23.0 cm
3 in = 7.5 cm	10 in = 25.5 cm
4 in = 10.0 cm	11 in = 28.0 cm
5 in = 12.75 cm	12 in = 30.5 cm
6 in = 15.25 cm	

1 ft = 30.5 cm	1 yd = 0.9 m
2 ft = 61.0 cm	
3 ft = 91.5 cm	

Area (approx)
1 yd^2 = 0.836 m^2

Weight (approx)
1 cwt = 50.8023 kg
1 ton UK = 1.02 tonnes

Introduction

On every account, and from every moral, intellectual and emotional point of view, it is in the best interest of all mortals to take joy and glory in a rock garden.
Reginald Farrer

Apart from those in some of the great botanic gardens and a few of the remaining large private or national gardens, the massive rock garden is a thing of the past. We are now in the era of small gardens, individually tended by enthusiastic amateurs and, for such environments, alpine plants are ideally suited.

Traditionally, anyone wishing to grow a collection of alpine plants was faced with the initial, and often Herculean, task of providing an appropriate environment in the form of a rock garden. Where this is feasible, it is still desirable, but those who hesitate on the brink of 'having a go' may console themselves with the knowledge that a proper rock garden is far from being an essential factor in the cultivation and enjoyment of these fascinating and endearing plants.

Alpine plants owe their popularity to their often exquisite beauty, their small size and the fact that a great many can be grown in a very small area. In short, they lend themselves admirably to the sort of intimate, do-it-yourself gardening which is becoming increasingly fashionable today. Most of the plants present no serious cultural problems and those which do offer a welcome challenge to those who have become captivated by their infinite variability and charm.

What are alpine plants?
This question is frequently asked of people like myself, who are supposed to know something about them. The answer would appear to be: 'A plant which comes from an alpine environment', but it is not so simple. A great many plants which are generally classified as 'alpines' have never seen a mountain but nevertheless fit into the conditions provided in gardens for plants of a mountain character and requirements. Some species of alpines can be found growing at sea-level and also at

great altitudes in mountainous regions, e.g. the lovely vernal gentian, *Gentiana verna*, which grows in meadows in the north of England, on the Burran in Eire and also high in the European Alps. Similarly, *Eritrichium nanum*, which is regarded as the archetypal alpine plant, grows at high altitudes in the Alps, but is also found at sea-level in Greenland.

One of the characteristics of a typical alpine from great altitudes is its dense, hummocky habit of growth, with tiny stems and wee rosettes of leaves condensed into domes and cushions. *Lepidium nanum* displays exactly these characters, but grows below sea-level in an alkaline North American desert!

Neither will stature alone qualify a plant as an alpine. In the same alpine or sub-alpine meadow in which grows *Gentiana verna*, you may find stately *G. lutea*, which achieves as many feet in height as *verna* does inches. Among the saxifrages, there are cushion-forming types, whose gay, stemless flowers sit tightly on compressed domes of hard leaves, and others which carry their flowers boldly on foot-high stems or in graceful, arching plumes nearly a yard in length.

It is obvious, therefore, that 'alpine' is no more than a loose and very general term to describe plants suitable for growing in the simulated alpine conditions which we try to provide in our gardens.

Where do alpine plants come from?

The wild species, subspecies and forms which are the *crème de la crème* of alpine plants are widely distributed over the temperate regions of the world. In such regions we can find plants from immense altitudes in the Himalayas, the Andes of South America, the high mountains of New Zealand and Australia, the Rocky Mountains of North America, the Atlas Mountains of North Africa—and even the Drakensberg mountains of South Africa, as well as from all the European ranges. The marvellous thing about a temperate climate is its ability to support exotic plants from other climes. In fact, in such a climate, plants can be grown from both the Tropics and the Arctic regions of the world.

A great many of the plants we grow as alpines have been garden-produced and, in the form in which they are grown, do not exist as wild plants anywhere. All the colourful aubrietias, for example, are selected hybrid seedlings. There are wild species of *Aubrieta*, but they do not match in beauty the garden-raised clones which make such a splendid spring display. Similarly the sun-roses, *Helianthemum*, are nearly all selected cultivars, although there are also some very desirable species. The brilliantly colourful strains of *Lewisia*, which are now so widely popular, have evolved by hybridisation between the original species, few of which are now grown. The few true species we still have are the intensely moral ones which refuse to hybridise!

There is quite a strong relict flora of alpine plants in the British Isles, e.g. *Alchemilla alpina, Betula nana, Dryas octopetala, Gentiana verna, Linnaea borealis, Minuartia verna, Primula farinosa, Pulsatilla vulgaris (= Anemone), Primula farinosa, Saxifraga oppositifolia, Silene acaulis*, many of which also occur in mountain regions of other countries. Of course, on no account should they be collected from their scattered habitats, except perhaps, and even then in moderation, as seeds; most, however, exist as nursery-grown stocks which have been cultivated for many generations.

The natural habitats of wild alpines vary enormously; nevertheless they all have to contend with a similar climate. They are accustomed to a snow-cover lasting for several months, they receive abundant moisture as the snow melts and their brief growing season commences and their flowering and seeding has to be accomplished before the onset of another winter with its long resting period.

These conditions are rarely possible to imitate exactly, but plants can be persuaded to adapt to a lowland environment. To the many plants classified as 'alpines' which do not come from a truly alpine environment must be added the innumerable garden-raised clones, varieties and hybrids which might be better described as 'rock garden plants'. Indeed, probably 50% of the plants grown in rock gardens have never seen a mountain.

Soil requirements

Enthusiastic gardeners, anxious to embark upon a new aspect of their rewarding occupation may be discouraged to hear that alpines are 'difficult and temperamental'. This reputation is doubtless due to that minority of alpine plants which do require special skills and knowledge. However, given attention to a few simple and basic rules, the majority should present no problems at all.

The novice should avoid the lovely but sometimes temperamental denizens of high alpine areas until sufficiently experienced to accept the challenge they offer. The pictures and descriptions of such plants as *Eritrichium nanum, Ranunculus glacialis* and species of Aretian *Androsace* and *Dionysia* from Iran and Afghanistan may be tempting, but to attempt to grow them before learning as much as possible of their special requirements can lead only to disappointment and discouragement.

Drainage

The one essential is good drainage. Alpines will not tolerate sour and sodden soil. They like plenty of water, but it must pass rapidly through the soil and not create a bog around their roots. If the natural soil where alpines are to be grown is clay, and especially if the site is level, it will be necessary to dig a few deep sump-holes and to fill them with some form of rough drainage, such as broken stone, brick or coarse cinders, so that surplus moisture can soak away and not collect around the roots of the plants. On a sloping site, it is easier to provide drainage by digging a few channels down-hill, filling these with similar materials.

Lime

Alpine plants fall into two major categories: those which like, or will tolerate, lime, and those which must have neutral or acid soil. The lime-haters are very particular in their requirements, but most of the lime-lovers will tolerate lime-free conditions. For example, nearly all types of *Dianthus* and *Aubrieta* are confirmed lime-lovers, but will thrive well enough without it. On the other hand, all the Asiatic autumn-flowering gentians, of which *Gentiana sino-ornata* is the classic example, and all members of the Ericaceae, such as *Cassiope*, *Rhododendron* and most heathers, require much more careful attention and will not survive in alkaline soils.

Compost

However, for the majority of alpines, no complicated soil mixture is required. A good standard compost can be prepared by mixing two parts of loam—or good top-spit garden soil, one part of fine-grade moss peat—or leaf mould, and one part of sharp sand or fine grit (all parts are by bulk). When the ingredients are assembled, and before they are mixed, a generous sprinkling of bonemeal will be a valuable addition. No other fertilizer is needed. Variations on the above mixture can be prepared for plants with special requirements. High alpines, for example, prefer a more gritty compost and, for these, the quantity of sand or grit can be increased.

Where to grow alpine plants

Although a rock garden is the ideal environment, alpine plants can be grown in a variety of other situations.

Aspect

Most alpine plants are sun-lovers, but there are exceptions. Such plants as *Ramonda*, *Haberlea*, some *Primula* spp., *Cassiope*, *Gaultheria* and *Vaccinium* prefer a modicum of shade or a cool north aspect.

Ideally, a rock garden should be situated in the open, away from any shade and possible drip from overhanging trees and on a gentle south or south-western slope. Such a site may not always be available but, as long as the situation is open and the drainage good, other aspects can be used, although if possible, it is best to avoid an aspect facing to the cold and unsympathetic east.

Rock gardens

To construct a rock garden is a somewhat laborious and certainly expensive operation. If a local stone is available it is likely to be cheaper — and a local stone should always be used in preference to an imported rock which might prove to be out of context. Moreover, imported rock, used in the neighbourhood of large towns, may well be affected by impurities in the air. In any case, the cost of transporting heavy rocks from one place to another is likely to be rather more than the cost of the material. However, if labour is available to help with the moving of heavy stones, and if these can be obtained at a reasonable price, a rock garden is well worth the effort.

The actual construction can be a 'do-it-yourself' task or you can employ an expert. The latter course involves considerable expense and there is always more pleasure and satisfaction to be gained from creating something oneself.

However small the rock garden, use reasonably large rocks—as large as can be comfortably handled. Pieces weighing from $\frac{1}{2}$–2 cwt can be moved without too much strain. By using a sack-truck running on planks, quite large and heavy rocks can be moved with no great effort. If a few basic rules are remembered, a satisfying result is not difficult to achieve.

The rocks should blend together either in outcrops or continuous building. Do not lay them in isolated splendour or put them on their smallest ends so that they stand up like pinnacles. Rocks should always be placed with a slight backward tilt and the joints between them should be flush or slightly overlapping. The strata of the outcrops should always tilt in one direction. Outcrops falling in different directions will never look right. Bury every rock used so that its base cannot be seen.

The amount of rock required will depend to some extent upon the building style adopted, but a site measuring say 150 ft^2 can be made into an attractive rock garden by using from 2 to 3 tons of stone in weights as previously suggested. Additional soil will, of course, be required to fill the outcrops as they are constructed and, as an approximate guide, 1 yd^3 of compost will be needed for each ton of rock. This compost should be mixed and ready for use when building commences. Its composition is given on p.10. This will answer the needs of the majority of alpine plants. For any special plants, separate composts can be mixed for individual 'pockets'.

A properly constructed rock garden provides a great many cracks, crannies and crevices between the rocks, and these form ideal homes for plants such as *Sempervivum*, *Lewisia*, *Saxifraga*, small *Dianthus*, *Saponaria*, *Gypsophila* and *Sedum*. A few of these should be at hand so that they can be put into place during the course of building, as it is not easy to plant in a narrow crevice once building has been completed.

Cracks and crannies

Not all gardens or circumstances permit the construction of a rock garden. Of the several other environments in which alpine plants will flourish, the cracks and crannies between paving stones offer just the conditions most alpines appreciate. Their roots will be in cool, moist soil beneath the paving-stones, their heads will be in the light, and their stems will be protected from a collar of wet soil. They will also relieve the monotonous flatness of a paved area.

Suitable plants for this purpose will be found listed at the end of the book. Do not be afraid to put in a few plants which grow in an upright rather than in a flat fashion. Even one or two slow-growing dwarf conifers would be quite appropriate.

As paving-stones are often laid upon cinders, sand or some other unsympathetic material, the planting positions should be excavated and filled with good compost so that the plants can get a good start. Once established, they will send their roots far and wide in search of nourishment. If the joints between the paving-stones have been cemented, it is usually possible to break away a corner here and there to provide an adequate planting position.

Walls

Another excellent habitat for alpine plants is in the cracks and crannies between the bricks or stones of a wall. It is, of course, easier to put in the plants as the wall is being built, but an old wall can usually be colonised, if not by actual plants, then by mixing the seeds of alpines with damp sand and dropping it into the crevices. There will be a considerable mortality but enough will survive to begin the colonisation. In due course there will be self-sown seedlings.

Walls can be retaining, built against a bank to hold up differing levels, or free-standing and two-sided, built hollow, with the centre filled with soil. The latter provides a number of aspects, as both the sides, the top and the ends of the wall can be used for a diversity of plants. One side may be sunny and the other shaded, which provides the opportunity for an even wider choice of species. I know of places, for which a rock garden was not thought appropriate, where several walls, of both types, have been built and these not only house a very wide collection of alpine plants but are also extremely decorative and economical of space.

Containers

Old stone troughs and sinks were first used as homes for alpine plants many years ago by the late Clarence Elliott, in his then famous nursery at Stevenage, Hertfordshire, in the British Isles. It is now a very popular method, but genuine old containers are becoming collector's pieces and are hard to come by. However, they are occasionally to be found and are invaluable for standing in patios and on paved areas near the house.

The old type of glazed kitchen sink may be a rather unsightly object in the garden, but its appearance can be improved by coating it with a mixture known as *hypertufa*. This consists of equal parts of fine grade peat, sharp sand and cement, mixed with water to the consistency of stiff dough. The smooth glazed surface should first be scored with some sharp implement. The surface to be covered is then painted with a bonding material which is allowed to become tacky. The hypertufa is then laid on to a thickness of about $\frac{1}{2}$ in and the surface is left rough. This will set hard in about 10 days and, as it becomes covered with moss and lichens, will eventually take on the appearance of stone. The weathering process can be hastened by painting on either water in which rice has been boiled or manure water. Both of these provide a slightly glutinous surface to which moss and lichen spores readily attach themselves.

Tufa rock

Tufa is a comparatively soft and very porous material into which holes can easily be bored, and seedlings and small plants can be set. As the plants become established, their roots penetrate the porous rock and they grow into characteristically hard and compact specimens. A sizeable piece of tufa can be bored with a great many such holes and can become a feature of great beauty and interest. It can be stood on paving or, preferably, by removing one paving-stone, set an inch or two into the ground. This encourages the absorption of water by capillary action so that overhead watering is needed less frequently.

Small pieces of this useful stone are invaluable for making up the miniature mountain-scapes which make sink and trough gardens so attractive. Although a limestone, tufa is a form called magnesian lime which does not lock up iron, enabling lime-haters to be grown in it quite happily. Even the small pieces can be drilled to contain individual plants, which enlarges the scope in even the smallest miniature garden.

If all else fails there is no reason why an area in the garden should not be excavated to a depth of 12 to 18 in and filled with alpine compost, perhaps made extra gritty to provide 'scree' conditions. A few flat stones partially sunk here and there provide easy access and there are a great many alpines which will be quite content in such an environment.

The alpine-house

As experience is gained and interest widens, the time will inevitably come when an alpine-house becomes necessary. An alpine-house can play a very important part in an alpine gardener's life as it provides the opportunity to grow many plants which are not altogether happy in the open, especially during unpredictable winters, and to enjoy a close association with plants when outdoor conditions may be unpleasant. Also the plants are accommodated at a convenient working level which appeals greatly to those who, with advancing age but no lack of gardening enthusiasm, find that the ground is uncomfortably far away!

Ideally, an alpine-house should be purpose-built and some greenhouse manufacturers specialise in their construction. The house should have a low 'pitch', to bring the plants as near as possible to the glass and continuous ventilation along both sides of the roof and of the sides at staging level; preferably, it should run north and south, with the door at the south end.

However, an ordinary green-house can be adapted and will serve very well. Additional ventilators can usually be inserted at no great expense and a steeper 'pitch' is not a serious drawback. The target is the maximum of light and air.

There are two schools of thought regarding heating in an alpine-house. Some gardeners like to be able to exclude frost. Others prefer to have no form of artificial heating, an important point when fuels and energy are so expensive. It is best not to grow alpines with other greenhouse plants which require very different conditions, although it is possible.

Pots and pans in an alpine-house can either stand on solid staging covered with ashes or shingle, or be sunk into staging built like a box and filled with sand or fine ash as a plunging medium. In the latter case, less watering is required, but the plants will tend to send out roots from the drainage holes in the bases of the containers. This can be a disadvantage, especially if the plants are moved at all regularly.

The watering can is the most important tool involved in caring for plants in an alpine-house, and, in unskilled hands, it can be a dangerous weapon. It has been said, with some justification, that more plants are killed by injudicious watering than by any other means. The safe rule to observe, when deciding if water is needed or not, is: 'If in doubt, don't'. A plant which has been over-saturated will seldom recover, whereas one which has been kept too dry will usually revive. During the winter months, when many plants are at rest, watering should be minimal, but at any time a mere splash is quite inadequate. When you water, water thoroughly, ensuring that the moisture reaches down to the bottom of the container, where most of the roots will be.

Plants which more or less demand the conditions provided by an alpine-house and others which, although growing well enough in the open, make a valuable contribution when grown in pots and pans, are listed at the end of the book.

Propagation

Seeds
Alpine plants, apart from sterile hybrids, produce seeds in great abundance. Pure species, generally, but not invariably, produce identical offspring. However, there are often variants among the progeny, some of which may even be superior in garden value to the parent. Some hybrids are fertile and their seeds will also provide plants with varying characteristics. One can choose the most desirable variants and propagate them vegetatively.

Plants which are usually grown as named clones of garden origin, e.g. *Aubrieta* and *Helianthemum*, should, unless one is seeking new forms, be vegetatively increased to maintain true stocks. There are good strains

15

of *Aubrieta* which can be raised from seed, but a mixture of colours will result, usually very decorative, but it is often desirable to perpetuate a particular colour; for this, one must take cuttings from, or divide, the particular clone.

Although the seeds of most alpine plants retain their viability for a considerable time, it is safer to sow them as soon as possible or convenient after ripening. This applies in particular to seeds of *Primula*, *Ranunculus* and *Lewisia*. If at all possible, these should be sown 'from pod to pot'. Seeds which are not, or cannot be, sown at once, should be stored in a cool, dry place until sowing is possible.

All alpine seeds benefit from being exposed to frost after sowing. If the pots, pans or boxes in which they have been sown are kept in an unheated green-house or cold frame, they will be frozen during cold winter weather. This is all to the good and it is remarkable to observe how rapidly they will germinate after such treatment. If no such cover is available, they can be stood outside on an ash or sand base and covered with glass or plastic. Some seeds are ready for sowing whilst still apparently unripe. This applies particularly to seeds of *Ranunculus* and *Lewisia*, which will fall whilst still green. Other plants are deceptive, such as the campanulas, many of which open their seed capsules at the back.

There are certain seeds, such as those of the pasque flower, *Pulsatilla (= Anemone) vulgaris*, and *P. (= A.) alpina* and several *Erodium*, which carry their seeds in a tiny pocket at the base of a long awn. It is well worth the extra trouble to sow seeds like these, not by laying them flat on the surface of the soil and covering them, but by spearing them individually into the compost. If you watch them on a dry, sunny day, you may observe the long awn actually coiling and driving the seeds deeper into the soil by what is known as hygrometrical action.

After many experiments I have found that seeds which are encased in a flat membrane, like those of most lilies and some gentians, will germinate better if sown on edge rather than flat. This entails the rather tedious operation of cutting tiny trenches into the compost with a thin piece of wood or metal, dropping individual seeds into the cut thus made and afterwards sifting over enough fine soil to cover them completely.

Alpine seeds can be sown with confidence on a proprietary seed compost, or a compost can be made up. This should resemble the standard mixture, with additional sand or fine, sharp grit, and should be passed through a rather fine sieve. Provide ample drainage in the container and fill it to within about $\frac{1}{2}$ in of the top, pressing it firm and level. Conventionally, seeds can be sown straight onto this surface and covered with a thin layer of soil—with the exception of course, of the awned or flat seeds.

Some alpine seeds take a long time to germinate. (I never throw a pot of alpine seeds away in less than 3 years and have often been surprised to discover a splendid germination even after such a lengthy period.) With very fine seeds, it is more satisfactory to cover the surface of the prepared container with a thin layer of pure washed grit and to sow directly onto this without any additional covering. Watering with a fine-rosed can will wash the seeds down into the grit. This has the advantage of preventing the growth of moss or liverwort on the surface of the soil, which frequently happens if germination is delayed, making it extremely difficult to extract and handle the tiny seedlings.

Seeds of many ericaceous plants, such as *Rhododendron*, *Erica*, *Vaccinium*, *Gaultheria*, are best sown on a compost composed of finely sifted peat and sharp sand or grit in equal quantities. They can also be sown onto a bed of fine grit.

As soon as the seeds germinate they should be exposed to full light and air; they will be ready for pricking off separately as soon as the true leaves appear between the cotyledons, or seed leaves. It is wise to sow seeds thinly to avoid overcrowding in the seed pan. It is not always possible to handle the seedlings promptly but they will not suffer if they have space in which to develop. In emergencies they may even be left in the seed pan until they are large enough for final potting.

Cuttings
Most alpine plants can be propagated from cuttings which are commonly made from young, sappy shoots or growth tips. Follow the normal procedure for cuttings, by severing them from the parent, removing the lower leaves with a sharp knife and making a final cut just below a node. Most commercial propagation by cuttings is now undertaken in mist units, but these are seldom available in the amateur's green-house, although small units can be installed at no considerable expense if desired.

Insert the cuttings into pure sand, or a mixture of sand and a small quantity of fine peat, water well and place the container in a close frame or in a small propagator. It is helpful first to dip the base of the cuttings into a hormone powder or liquid, preferably containing a fungicide. Such preparations are available from most garden centres or horti-

17

cultural suppliers. Should no frame or propagator be available, the container can be placed in a polythene bag and sealed; remember to open it occasionally to admit air and remove the condensation.

Cuttings of dwarf alpine shrubs, such as *Daphne*, *Rhododendron* and others which make more woody growth, are usually taken when the growths are firm and semi-ripened. These may be pulled off with a tiny heel of older wood, which should be neatly trimmed with a sharp knife or cut below a leaf node.

Division
Established plants of many alpines can be increased by dividing them into small, rooted portions, an operation best carried out early in the year or in the late summer and early autumn. Such divisions are usually potted until they have become established and have made good roots before being planted in their permanent positions. However, in good weather, the divisions can be planted, if they are adequately supplied with roots, straight into the open. Make sure that they are kept moist during dry weather and, in very hot sunlight, give them some form of shading.

All alpines, except those which grow from a central crown or tap-root, can be divided. For the latter, one must rely upon cuttings or seeds, although, in some cases, stems and branches which spread out close to the ground will root as they go and can be detached and treated as individuals. It is also possible to induce self-layering. *Daphne cneorum*, for example, is apt to make rather long and often almost leafless stems. If these are covered with a sandy, peaty compost, right up to the leafy tips, they will usually make roots and can eventually be detached and grown as separate plants.

Grafting
This method of propagation is not often practised by alpine gardeners as there are few plants which call for it. The notable exceptions are the rarer *Daphne*, some of which do not root easily from cuttings nor provide generous quantities of seed. The classic example is probably *D. petraea*, which is difficult to root, does not seed and, curiously enough, is often rather shy-flowering if grown in cultivation as a rooted cutting. There is no logical explanation for this behaviour but experience has proved that grafted plants are more satisfactory. Although it is very often grafted onto stocks of *D. mezereum*—and successfully—I prefer

to use a stock which is evergreen as it seems wrong to graft an ever-green plant onto a deciduous one. *D. mezereum* is also given to sucker-ing, which is another reason why a species such as *D. retusa*, or any evergreen species of which seedlings are available, is preferable as a stock.

There are various methods of grafting, but, for *Daphne*, or any other shrubby alpine plants, I find it simplest to select a stock and cut it off clean about 1 in from the ground. A clean cut downward in the centre of the stock should then be made, about $\frac{1}{4}$ in in depth. The scion is made from a ripened shoot of the plant to be grafted; its stem should be cleaned of leaves and cut with a very sharp knife to a wedge shape at the base. This sliver is then gently inserted into the cut in the stock, ensuring that the bark on one side of the scion coincides with the bark on the stock.

The simplest method of securing the scion is to tie a piece of moistened raffia around the union. This should then be covered with grafting wax to exclude air and moisture. Grafted plants are best kept in a closed frame or box until there are signs that the scion is growing, after which they can be removed and given ordinary alpine-house or cool green-house treatment. The scions which have been used may contain dormant flower buds. It is best to remove these as they develop, not permitting the new plant to flower in its first year.

Pests and diseases
It is an unfortunate fact that plants are often subject to attack by aphids, insects and viruses, although, in my experience, alpine plants are less troubled than other plants by such problems.

Aphid
Infestations of aphids, green, black or white, can be controlled by using any one of the several standard remedies, e.g. dimethoate, lindane, malathion. Out-of-doors, these are applied by a spray of some kind, either in the form of an aerosol or through a pressure sprayer. For plants under glass I like to use a systemic killer if one can be found that is appropriate to the particular pest. In the green-house, containers of specific pesticides can be installed in the electrically operated heaters. The pesticides are gradually disseminated into the air and exercise a good measure of control. The unit required is, however, very expensive.

Red spider mite

One of the most difficult pests to control in an alpine-house is red spider mite, but even this will yield to aerosol or careful spray treatment with derris, dimethoate or malathion. With high alpine cushion plants, such as the rarer species of *Androsace*, *Draba* and similar soft-leaved, rosetted plants, the use of wet sprays can be disastrous and do more harm than the pest they are designed to exterminate.

Root aphid

Primulas, especially the European species, are particularly liable to attack by root aphid. I have found that the use of leaf mould in the compost encourages this pest and using moss peat instead greatly reduces the incidence of attack. In severe cases one should shake all the soil from the roots of afflicted plants and wash them in a solution of permethrin or malathion.

Vine weevil

This is another persistent pest, whose grubs in the soil can create enormous havoc. This can be controlled to some extent by the use of Nemesys in the potting compost. Remember always to follow the instructions on the containers. Never exceed the recommended proportions. With alpine plants, it is often best to err on the modest side and make the mixtures slightly weaker than recommended.

It may seem an unnecessary warning, but accidents do happen, and it is vitally important that all chemicals, many of which are highly toxic, should be kept in well marked containers and out of reach of children.

Descriptions

Figures in bold after an entry indicate plate numbers

Acaena [Rosaceae]

This genus of plants, mostly native to New Zealand, consists of vigorous and rapidly spreading plants which will lose no time in smothering any smaller neighbours. Completely unfussy about soil, they will grow in austere conditions and flourish with extra exuberance in richer composts. They are sun-lovers, but can be grown in light shade.

They are used mainly as carpeting ground-coverers, or for planting in crevices between paving stones. They make good cover for dwarf alpine bulbs and provide attractive ground cover when the bulbs are not in evidence. The species described below are in general cultivation and are the most valuable.

— *adscendens* is a carpeter, although not so prostrate as some. It forms a tangled mat of semi-woody stems, clothed in blue-grey leaves, toothed at the margins. As with nearly all acaenas, the individual flowers are inconspicuous and are carried in dense heads; in this species they are creamy-green in colour and the plant is to be regarded for its decorative foliage.

— *buchananii* is another prostrate spreader with dense mats of pea-green leaves and bristly flower heads of orange-brown.

— *glauca* has little floral value but its carpets of silky-haired grey-blue leaves make it desirable.

— *microphylla* is deservedly one of the most popular species. It is entirely prostrate, with prettily bronzed leaves and burr-like heads of tiny flowers interspersed with mingled scarlet bristles.

— *novae-zealandae* is slightly more robust and is one of the most vigorous spreaders. It leaves are felted with silky hairs and the flower heads are purple and spiky.

Acantholimon [Plumbaginaceae]

Certain species of *Acantholimon* are not easy to obtain, being as rare in cultivation as others are in nature. Their native haunts are Eastern Europe and still further eastward to Tibet. Avid sun-lovers, they relish hot, dry situations in perfectly drained soil.

— *glumaceum* is reasonably common and delightfully easy to grow. It can be found underfoot on

Mount Ararat and also occurs in the Caucasus Mountains. Its deep green, very narrow leaves are gathered into dense humps and cushions which are bedecked in summer with short sprays of pink flowers. Although *A. glumaceum* has been grown in our gardens since 1851, it was not until 1960 that it received its well deserved Award of Merit. It is easily propagated by division or cuttings.

— *venustum* hails from the Cilician Taurus, whence it first came in 1873 to be almost immediately given a First Class Certificate. Slow-growing, but not difficult, it is seen at its loveliest when grown as a specimen in a deep pot or pan in the alpine-house. The needle-fine, sharply pointed leaves are grey-green, in lax cushions which set off to great advantage the arching sprays of pink, papery bracts which shield the small flowers. It does not divide readily and is reluctant to root from cuttings.

Achillea [Compositae]

There are achilleas to please all tastes, from tall border plants to tiny mat-forming kinds, ideal for rock gardens, cracks in paving or crannies in sunny walls. None is difficult to grow, but they do relish an open, sunny position and, in common with all alpines, insist upon good drainage. Some have handsome flowers; others rely upon foliage effects for their impact and some combine the two virtues.

— *ageratifolia* is, by some authorities, said to be an *Anthemis* and not an *Achillea*. A Greek plant, it has narrow, silvered leaves, deeply toothed at the edges, and carries its large white-rayed flowers singly on 6 in stems.

— *aurea* is typically a reasonably attractive plant, making flat mats of emerald-green, rather ferny foliage over which stand flattened umbels of yellow flowers. It is, however, surpassed in desirability by a form, discovered by my late father, which grows on Mount Olympus in Greece. Here the leaves are grey-green and the blossoms more richly yellow in much larger umbels. It is a plant of the sunniest disposition, rapidly making foot-wide pads of its pretty foliage. It will be found as *A. a.* 'Grandiflora' in catalogues.

— *chrysocoma* comes from Dalmatia, Yugoslavia. Like the other species described, it is a tufty carpeter—although none need be feared as an invader—and the highly aromatic foliage is densely covered with grey hairs. The bright yellow flowers are borne in compact heads on 6 in stems.

— *clavennae* is a species of considerable distinction from Eastern Europe. Its leaves are oval in shape, irregularly toothed and brilliantly silvered with a pelt of

22

fine hairs. It is of bushy rather than mat-forming habit and carries its good white flowers boldly in clusters on 6–9 in stems.

— *fraasii* has been unjustly condemned as a plant of little garden value and it may not be all that easy to obtain. The flowers are admittedly of poor quality—I usually remove the flower stems before they develop fully, but the 1 ft-high mounds of filigree silver leaves are extremely decorative. It should be regarded primarily as a foliage plant.

— × *grisebachii* is a hybrid of uncertain parentage and of garden origin. It is mat-forming and has good silver leaves and heads of pure white flowers. It seldom exceeds 4 in in height, even when in flower.

— × *kellereri* is a hybrid claiming *A. clavennae* as one parent, the other being unknown. A good plant, it has delicately cut, very silver leaves and sizeable white flowers in loose heads on 6 in stems.

— 'King Edward' is a neat and tidy hybrid which occurred as a chance seedling in my father's nursery many years ago; he named it in honour of his then friend and patron, Hugh Lewis. It became known as × *lewisii* and still appears in some lists under this name. Curiously enough, the identical hybrid cropped up almost simultaneously in another garden and was named *A.* 'King Edward' by its discoverer. As the rule of priority obtains in plant nomenclature, the latter name must be regarded as correct.

— *tomentosa* is possibly the most frequently encountered alpine species. It spreads quickly into dense mats of finely cut and intensely hairy leaves, over which the yellow flowers are carried in large umbels on short stems. By no means an aristocrat, it is a very useful plant, presenting no problems of cultivation or propagation.

— × *wilczekii* is rather more robust. It is of hybrid origin and is popular with those who have a fondness for silver-leaved plants. It forms loose tufts of saw-edged, very silvery leaves and the white flowers are borne on slightly drooping panicles.

All the above are likely to blossom in late spring and summer and some may well continue to produce flowers into early autumn. They can all be increased without difficulty by division and those which are not of hybrid origin can be raised from seed.

Acorus [Araceae]

Of the two species of *Acorus*, only *A. gramineus* is of interest to rock gardeners. The type itself is of little value, but there are two forms, 'Pusillus' and 'Variegatus', which are of interest even if not beautiful. The first is a 2-in miniature tuft of grassy leaves with a liking for a moist situation and the second, the better of the two, has narrow, grassy leaves with striped bands of green and white.

Adenophora [Campanulaceae]

Few of these close cousins of *Campanula* are native to Europe; they are confined mostly to Japan and China, with one or two in Siberia. Some fifteen species are in cultivation, but only a few are available commercially. Others are grown in private collections and in botanic gardens. Those listed below are most likely to be available and suitable, but may be considered a trifle tall for a small rock garden; however, they are useful plants for the front of a flower border, easily grown and summer-flowering.

— *bulleyana* is one of the tallest in this genus and its stems can tower to 3 ft. They branch terminally and display clusters of large, deep lavender-blue bells.

— *confusa* (=*farreri*) is also quite tall and the leafy stems end in branching panicles of blue bells.

— *nikoensis* is one of the dwarfer species, seldom topping 1 ft in height; its clear pale blue flowers are very attractive.

— *takedai* and *tashiroi* are both Japanese and are very worthwhile. The former has rather weak, but fairly tall stems and deep blue flowers. The latter is dwarfer, varying between 5 and 10 in, and

its deep violet-blue flowers are quite beautiful.

Adonis [Ranunculaceae]

Although not strictly alpine plants, at least two species are frequently planted on rock gardens, where they are to be especially appreciated for their brightly coloured flowers, produced very early in the year. Given congenial weather they will blossom in early March, coinciding with the departure of the snowdrops. They flourish in any good garden soil and will accept sun or light shade and may be increased by division of old plants, or raised from seed.

— *vernalis* is European and appears first as a low tuft of deeply cleft leaves over which, on short stems, gleam large yellow multipetalled flowers.

— *volgensis* came to us from the USSR and can be thought of as a slightly more robust *A. vernalis*, a little larger in all its parts.

Aethionema [Cruciferae]

These invaluable dwarf, slightly shrubby, plants come mostly from regions with long days of warm sunshine in the Mediterranean and eastward into Asia Minor. Their chosen habitats indicate their liking for warm and sunny positions. Although lime-lovers, they will all tolerate neutral or even acid soils. They flower abundantly from early summer onward.

Propagation is not difficult. Soft growth tips, taken before flower buds have been formed, root easily and they can also be raised from the seeds they produce in abundance. I count them amongst the most desirable of semi-shrubby rock garden plants.

— *armenum* comes from Armenia. Its short, branching, woody stems are clothed with small, narrow, green leaves and the pink flowers are displayed in terminal racemes.

— *cordatum* is a rarity from the Lebanon, forsaking family tradition and carrying clusters of small, sulphur-coloured flowers. It is not very easy to obtain.

— *coridifolium* (= *jucundum*) is a pleasant enough woody bush, up to 9 in in height, with glaucous foliage and rose-lilac flowers, but it is surpassed in beauty and garden value by a trinity of hybrids. The original appeared many years ago as a chance seedling in the then famous garden of the late Ellen Willmott at Warley, Essex, in the British Isles, and was named 'Warley Hybrid'. It was compact in habit and bore showers of pink flowers. Since then it has been superseded by two selections, one named 'Warley Rose' and the other 'Warley Ruber'. They are both good, but the last named is of superlative beauty. It is as handsome as a dwarf *Daphne* and has flowers of the richest possible rose-red. Seed is seldom produced

but cuttings root very easily. 1

— *grandiflorum* first came to us, in 1879, from the Lebanon and Iran and has long been treasured as a splendidly decorative plant. It gained the coveted Award of Garden Merit of the Royal Horticultural Society as long ago as 1938. It makes a 1 ft high bushlet of tangled woody stems, carrying racemes of flowers, the colour of pink coconut ice, from May until late summer.

— *pulchellum* is not unlike *A. grandiflorum* in its habit of growth. It is a nice, mounded bushlet of grey-green leaves, smothered in summer with rich pink flowers.

— *rotundifolium* asks for, and deserves, alpine-house treatment. It is probably more correctly named *Eunomia oppositifolia*. It comes from Syria and has semi-prostrate, rather fleshy stems, set with similarly fleshy grey leaves of waxy texture and ending in heads of quite large white or softly pink flowers.

Ajuga [Labiatae]

Although the bugles are not in any way 'alpine' plants, they are often grown on and around rock gardens, although they are most useful as ground coverers between and beneath shrubs and trees. They appreciate a modicum of shade or a cool aspect. Those most likely to be grown are forms of the British *A. reptans* and selected forms have been given clonal names. The wild type, really too rampageous for gardens, may have blue, pink or white flowers in leafy short spikes over the green foliage, but more desirable are those with coloured foliage, such as 'Rainbow', 'Multicolor' and 'Atropurpurea'. These all have flowers in some shade of blue or purple, and there is a very dwarf, green leaved form with pink flowers known as 'Pink Elf'. There also exists a curious *Ajuga*, often listed as *A. metallica* 'Crispa', which has been attributed to both *A. genevensis* and *A. pyramidalis*. It makes tight, ground-hugging huddles of crisped and crimped dark green leaves and carries blue flowers in very short racemes.

Alchemilla [Rosaceae]

None of the several species of *Alchemilla* is of startling floral beauty but a few are well worth growing for the sake of their pretty leaves. They will grow almost anywhere and in any soil and, with a few exceptions, are too robust to be trusted near less vigorous plants.

— *alpina* is a pleasant little alpine species, handsome in rock crevices and crannies. Its divided leaves are green above and gleaming silver on the undersides. Its greenish-yellow tiny flowers are unimportant.

— *erythropoda* is a comparative newcomer from Eastern Europe. Its tufts of softly hairy grey leaves, surmounted by clouds of tiny, soft yellow flowers never fail to attract admiration.

— *mollis* is a robust plant, able to spread far and wide by means of its myriad seeds. Use it as ground cover between shrubs, or as a wall plant. If allowed to riot in company with the equally rumbustuous *Campanula poscharskyana*, it will make a summer-long picture of great beauty. The rounded and jagged, hairy grey-green leaves of the alchemilla, and the innumerable sprays of chartreuse flowers, associate splendidly with the long trails of blue flowers produced by the campanula. Its hairy leaves trap drops of rain or dew and these glisten like diamonds in sunlight. 2

Allardia [Compositae]

A rarity which the enthusiastic collector should seek with eagerness, *A. tomentosa* was introduced many years ago from the high valleys of Kashmir but never took to cultivation sufficiently well to become widely available. If it can be obtained, it is definitely for the alpine-house, where it will make —if you are lucky, or sufficiently clever—a low mound of lacy, en-silvered leaves. As far as I know it has not yet produced in gardens its daisy-shaped flowers, which have pink rays and a yellow disc surrounded by a rim of brown.

Allium [Liliaceae]

There are some very beautiful alliums and many are dwarf enough to be highly desirable rock garden plants. The familiar odour of onions possessed by nearly all the species in this genus only becomes objectionable if and when they are roughly handled. Alliums vary in character from plants with true bulbs to others with swollen, bulbous bases. None of those included here is difficult to grow and all will be pleased with any good soil.

— *albopilosum* is more correctly known as *A. christophii*. Too large for most rock gardens, but a splendid border plant, it carries, on tall, naked stems, huge rounded umbels of flowers which are of a metallic purple colour. The dried flower heads are in considerable demand for winter decorations.

— *beesianum* is a tiny Chinese plant which, from tufts of fibrous rhizomes emits many narrow, fleshy leaves and short stems carrying pendant clusters of bright blue flowers.

— *caeruleum* (= *azureum*) comes from Russia and, on its 1 ft-high stems, offers crowded umbels of small, but clear blue flowers. It shares a common *Allium* habit of occasionally including among its flowers a few small bulbils from which new plants can be raised.

— *cyaneum* (= *purdomii*) is another Chinese plant. It makes neat tufts of grass-fine leaves and carries its clusters of cobalt-blue flowers on 6 in stems just above the foliage.

— *cyathophorum* 'Farreri' is similar in habit to the last named, but its flowers are wine-red in colour.

— *flavum* comes from Eastern Europe, and does not conform to the family pattern of blue or purple flowers but is bright yellow. The type is quite tall, but there is a charming miniature, *A.f.* 'Minus', which is never more than a few inches in height. It delights in a hot and dry situation.

— *karataviense* is very definitely a bulb and, from its fat tubers, spring pairs of wide, metallic-grey leaves and, from between these twin leaves, rise 9 in stems, ending in a globe of grey-lavender flowers. It is extremely decorative in both leaf and flower.

— *moly* is extremely invasive and can, if in the wrong place, or uncontrolled, become a nuisance— but a lovely one, for its rich golden flowers, carried on 12 in stems, are quite lovely. Let it colonise some piece of waste ground, even in the poorest soil and it will be enjoyable, but do not plant it on the rock garden.

— *narcissiflorum* (= *pedemontanum)* is one of the gems of the race and is a splendid rock garden plant. Its rhizomatous roots are covered in brown felt. It forms few leaves but the 6 in stems carry pendant bells of rich wine-red and are of goodly size.

— *neapolitanum* hails from Mediterranean regions and, in very cold districts, may prove slightly tender. In Italy, it is often grown for a cut flower, for the loose sprays of pure white flowers are decorative and slightly fragrant — not of onions!

— *ostrowskianum* is another treasure and a true bulb. Its narrow leaves appear in small tufts at ground level and on the 4 in stems are umbels of wide-petalled carmine-red flowers. There is a selected form, raised in Holland, named 'Zwanenburg' with flowers very rich in colour.

— *siculum* is rather tall, but cannot be excluded. When in flower the stems may be 3 ft tall and naked. Each stem carries a loose cluster of large, pendant, bell-shaped flowers of a curious blue-green colour, each petal being adorned by a narrow maroon stripe.

— *triquetrum* should be regarded with care as it can seed far and wide in the extent of becoming a slight nuisance. It is found in hedge-bottoms and roadsides in the western counties of the British Isles and has become naturalised, although originally introduced from Europe. It is a good inhabitant of cool, shady places where it freely produces its loose tufts of narrow leaves and, on triangular stems, umbels of pendant, bell-shaped flowers, pure white and slightly fragrant, each petal with a clear green stripe.

Alopecurus [Gramineae]

Some alpine grasses take too kindly to cultivation and become intolerable nuisances in a rock garden, but not *A. lanatus*, which is a dwarf Spanish grass with leaves of hoary-grey. It is a pleasant plant to grow in a dry and sunny position and adds to its attractions when it bears on short stems the flowerlets in white, woolly bundles.

Alyssum [Cruciferae]

All alyssums are sun and lime-lovers and magnificent wall plants. There are no white-flowered alyssums; these are really ptilotrichums.

— *montanum* from Central Europe and the Caucasus is a spreading mat of woody stems and hairy grey leaves with heads of fragrant, soft yellow flowers. It varies from being absolutely prostrate to a slightly more bushy habit up to 6 in tall.

— *murale* is little more than an annual, but is useful for providing a massed display of lemon-yellow flowers. It can grow to a height of about 1 ft and, if it does not seed itself, is easily raised from seed.

— *saxatile* is the most commonly grown rock garden alyssum and, in its several forms, makes a brave display in the early spring, along with the aubrietias. Use them in moderation. There is a temptation to make great drifts but once they have finished flowering one is left with large flowerless areas for the rest of the year. The forms to seek are 'Citrinum', 'Compactum' and 'Dudley Neville'. The latter has flowers of an attractive orange-buff colour. After their spring display they benefit from a gentle 'hair-cut'. This maintains them in a neat and compact habit and prolongs their useful life.

— *serpyllifolium* is a Spaniard and particularly neat and desirable. It is quite prostrate, its thin, woody stems spreading horizontally. The tiny leaves are grey-green and the flower heads yellow. It is small enough to be grown in a stone sink or trough.

— *spinosum* see *Ptilotrichum*.

All the above can be propagated from seeds or cuttings, but the forms of *A. saxatile* must be vegetatively propagated as they do not breed true from seed.

Anacyclus [Compositae]

Coming from the Atlas Mountains of North Africa, *A. depressus*, as one would expect from its habitat, is an inveterate sun lover. It grows easily in sharply gritty soil in the open and is also a handsome specimen plant for a pot or pan in the alpine-house. From a deeply delving root radiate horizontal stems carrying finely cut leaves; each one ends in a daisy flower, the ray florets being white on the upper side and crimson beneath. The contrast of the white flowers and not yet expanded crimson buds with the grey-green ferny foliage is exquisite.

Anagallis [Primulaceae]

— *arvensis* is the well known British scarlet pimpernel, or poor man's weatherglass. It is a plant to be enjoyed in the wild, not a garden plant, but there are one or two exotic species which are very desirable.

— *linifolia* comes from the warmer parts of Europe and spreads into North Africa. Its semi-trailing, spreading, leafy stems form wide mats and are smothered in summer beneath myriads of rounded flowers of rich gentian-blue. Plants named *A. collina*, *A. phillipsii* or *A. monellii* should be regarded as belonging to *A. linifolia*, which is an aggregate species. These may be blue or bright red. They are sun-lovers and sometimes short-lived and, if grown out-of-doors, may suffer in a severe winter. A plant or two should be kept under cover as an insurance. They are easily reproduced from seeds or cuttings.

— *tenella* has different requirements. It is another British native, known as the bog pimpernel, and chooses moist places in which to grow. An especially fine form, originally found in Dorset in the British Isles, and named *A. t.* 'Studland' is a charmer and grows flat on the ground in mats of soft green leaves smothered with innumerable, stemless, clear pink, honey-scented flowers.

Anchusa [Boraginaceae]

In general, anchusas are tall border plants and only one species qualifies as an alpine. It is a treasure from the mountains of Crete, known as *A. caespitosa*. It should be given a deep bed of gritty, humus-rich soil and an open, sunny situation, or grown in deep pots in the alpine-house. On the whole it seems happiest in the open. Its vigorous and deeply delving root produces a ground-hugging cluster of leathery, narrow, dark-green leaves with undulating margins. Each rosette is centred by almost stemless flowers of deep, clear blue. There is an imposter which sometimes usurps its name, a much taller plant, correctly called *A. angustissima*.

Andromeda [Ericaceae]

Generally the andromedas are too tall for rock gardens but *A. polifolia* provides a few fascinating miniature shrubs. They demand lime-free soil and a north aspect or cool position in light shade and are ideal peat-garden plants. A rare British native, this species is also distributed through Central and Northern Europe. It grows to a height of about 18 in, with woody stems clothed in small, hard, leathery leaves. The pink, bell-shaped flowers are carried in small clusters at the tips of the shoots. The more desirable forms are 'Compacta', 'Major' and 'Minor', which are dwarfer and more compact, and there is one charmer with pure white flowers.

Androsace [Primulaceae]

This large and important genus contains some of the choicest and most desirable alpine plants. Some are easy to grow; others offer a challenge to skilled and knowledgeable cultivators. In nature they are distributed widely in Europe and roam into Asia and North America. Their requirements are variable. They are mostly propagated from seed, but some yield cuttings which can be rooted. They are spring- and early summer-flowering and all, regardless of their individual needs, demand really sharply drained soil. Their composts should be generously supplied with sharp sand or fine grit.

— *alpina* (=*glacialis*) must be regarded as an intractable plant. It really qualifies, along with *Eritrichium nanum*, as one of the few alpines which stubbornly refuse to adapt themselves to lowland conditions. Just occasionally, an exceptionally skilful cultivator proudly displays a living specimen on the show benches, but never in the glory to be seen on the highest screes of the Alps in Europe. If you would like to try — and can obtain a young plant or a seedling, give it lime-free soil made up as a sort of gritty detritus with humus in it. It accepts moisture in abundance early in the year, when it is accustomed to being saturated by melting snow. You may hopefully expect, but will seldom achieve, close mats of softly hairy shoots and leaves covered by innumerable clear pink flowers. It is one of the glories of the high mountains but a classic garden failure.

— *carnea* is a pretty and easily grown plant, on the other hand. It lacks the pure aristocracy of *A. alpina*, but has its own beauty, when the cushions of tiny, rather dark green leaves are starred by heads of pink—or occasionally white, flowers carried in small heads on 2–3 in stems.

— *chamaejasme* is an inhabitant of turfy alpine meadows, where it likes close association with other plants—as do many alpines. It is commonly grown in solitary splendour in gardens without any great difficulty. The hairy, grey-green leaves are gathered into small rosettes, above which rise short stems bearing heads of flowers,

white when they first expand, but ageing to rose-pink, with a yellow eye.

— *charpentieri* is not one of the easiest plants to grow, but does yield to careful persuasion in gritty, humus-rich compost. It thrives best in the alpine-house. Its blunt leaves, covered with a pelt of fine hairs, form into neat rosettes and each short stem displays one rose-red flower.

— *ciliata* is one of the choice species, known as Aretians, which should be given alpine-house treatment. It comes from the Pyrenees and has tiny, flat leaves which build into humps of neat rosettes. On each of its short stems appear one or two rich pink, yellow-centred flowers. Like its fellows it is often resentful of overhead watering.

— *cylindrica* is another Aretian from the Pyrenees and asks for similar treatment. Its hummocks of grey-leaved rosettes carry almost stemless white or, occasionally, faintly pink flowers.

— *geranifolia* is from North India and Tibet and differs considerably in appearance from its European cousins. It displays loose tufts of slightly scalloped, rounded and hairy leaves and produces erect, rather wiry stems to a height of about 6 in, crowned with heads of soft pink flowers. Occasionally, as they mature, the flower heads bend over until they touch the soil and form roots, thus becoming separate individuals.

— *helvetica* can be classified as a typical high alpine cushion plant. One of the aristocrats of the Aretians, it is found, usually on limestone, in cracks and crannies on cliff faces in the Alps of Europe. It is very definitely an alpine-house species and will there make tightly huddled pads of tiny leaves compressed into tight rosettes, on which sit the stemless white, golden-eyed blossoms.

— *hirtella* is another Aretian, from the Pyrenees, very amenable to careful alpine-house cultivation and not nearly as sensitive as some of its kin. It has the softly hairy leaves typical of its group, again huddled into neat domes, studded with rounded white or, occasionally, soft pink flowers.

— *lactea* comes from the alpine meadows of Europe and is a happy and easy little plant forming loose tufts of rosetted, smooth leaves. Each 4–6 in stem carries a few white, yellow-eyed flowers. It is not long-lived, but provides plenty of seeds for easy continuity.

— *lanuginosa* is a Himalayan and of very different appearance. It delights in a sunny crevice, from which it trails its stems and en-silvered leaves. From the leaf axils spring clusters of pink flowers. There is a variety, *leichtlinii*, which is similar in habit, but the flowers are white, with a pink or yellow eye.

— *primuloides* now includes *A. sarmentosa* and various named clones, such as *chumbyi*, 'Salmon's Variety', *watkinsii* and *yunnanensis*. There is a close similarity between all of them; they differ only in the richness in colour of their pink or softly red flowers, which are carried in close heads on short stems above the clustered and mat-forming rosettes of hairy grey leaves. It grows well in the open, but in very wet winters appreciates being covered by a pane of glass.

— *pubescens* and *pyrenaica* both come from the Pyrenees and are Aretians of great merit as alpine-house plants. It has been known for them to survive, and even flourish, in holes drilled in a large tufa rock out-of-doors, but there is a considerable element of risk. They each make the tidiest and neatest of closely packed domes of tiny rosetted leaves and, in the spring, are concealed beneath myriads of the almost stemless, white flowers.

— *sempervivoides* is an easy outdoor species from the Himalayas. It has rosettes of smooth leaves rather like those of a *Sempervivum*, and, on short scapes, are many pink flowers.

— *strigillosa* strikes a different note in having quite large leaves, covered in a pelt of fine hairs and gathered into loose tufts and umbels of purple-pink flowers on 9–12 in stems. It can be grown outside, but is usually treated to alpine-house conditions. It is a Himalayan.

— *vandelli* is probably better known as either *A. imbricata* or *A. argentea*. It hails from granite rocks in the Central and Southern European Alps and makes dense pads and cushions of tightly packed silver-leaved rosettes of very small leaves. The whole plant disappears at flowering time beneath a wealth of stemless, neatly rounded, white, yellow-eyed flowers. It is an Aretian for the alpine-house.

— *villosa* inhabits not only Europe, but extends into Asia. It can be grown happily in the open in a sunny place and in very gritty soil. It makes loose mats of tufts of small, grey-green leaves carried at the ends of red stolons. The fragrant flowers are usually white, but can be soft pink with a deeper eye. There is a slightly more compact form, named *arachnoidea*, from the limestones of the Karawanken Mountains of Austria.

Andryala [Compositae]

Silver-leaved plants are always popular and *A. aghardii*, from Mediterranean regions, is a dwarf sub-shrub with woody stems ending in groups of narrow intensely silver leaves. In mid-summer it displays heads of yellow flowers on short stems. The whole plant seldom exceeds 1 ft in height and will appreciate all the sun it can get.

Anemone [Ranunculaceae]

— *alpina* see *Pulsatilla*.

— *apennina* and *blanda* both grow from tuberous rhizomes and are often sold as dry bulbs. They prefer positions which are cool and lightly shaded but are otherwise unfussy. Spring-flowering plants, they are commonly blue, in one of several shades but each is capable of producing forms with pink or white blossoms. No more than a few inches high they give a colourful display in a cool corner of the rock garden and are also useful as underplants for shrubs.

— *magellanica* comes from South America and is something of a Cinderella. Admittedly it has no startling beauty, but in its own quiet way it fills a useful niche. The tufts of basal leaves are deeply cleft and hairy and from them rise 6–9 in stems, bearing cream-white flowers. If something a little more imposing than the type is desired, try 'Major', which is slightly larger in all its parts and has flowers that are more cream than white.

— *nemorosa* is the wood anemone, to be admired in its native haunts in the British Isles but not really a garden plant. There are named forms which are quite lovely, such as *A. n.* 'Allenii', with its wide-petalled flowers of pale blue, *A. n.* 'Robinsoniana', whose flowers are larger and of a deeper blue and a special gem named 'Vestal', whose pure white saucers are centred with clusters of white filaments.

— *obtusiloba* looks more like a buttercup than an anemone and is, indeed, sometimes called the blue buttercup of Kashmir. Its lobed, softly hairy leaves make tufts from which radiate branching stems carrying beautifully rounded soft blue flowers. In its native Kashmir one can discover forms with cream, white and even yellow flowers, but few, if any, of these seem to be in cultivation.

— *palmata* can be found wild in Spain and Portugal. It is tuberous, with small lobed and rounded leaves and cup-shaped flowers of a good yellow. There are albino forms too and all will be the better for a warm, sheltered position.

— *ranunculoides* is also known as wood ginger, and is a rather frail woodlander from Europe and the Caucasus. It wanders here and there, gently and harmlessly, emitting toothed leaves and short wiry stems carrying cheerful yellow flowers in early spring. There are two forms, one with double flowers and another with bronzed leaves and larger flowers, known respectively as 'Pleniflora' and 'Superba'.

— *trifolia* is a delicacy which, if you happen to be in the woodlands at Misurina, in Italy, you may see, early in the year, proffering its flowers of soft, clear blue over leaves like those of *A. nemorosa*.

Antennaria [Compositae]

Rather unexciting but useful, this small family of prostrate ground-coverers, mostly with silver foliage and small, tufty heads of white, pink or red flowers, is valuable for carpeting the ground over alpine bulbs and for crevices between paving stones. Those most likely to please are all forms of *A. dioica*.

Antirrhinum [Scrophulariaceae]

There are few antirrhinums appropriate to rock gardens.

— *asarina* see *Asarina procumbens*
— *hispanicum* is a 1 ft-high bushy plant, with white, pink or purple flowers, for the alpine-house. It comes from Spain.
— *molle* from the Pyrenees, also asks for slight protection and is of similar character. Its large flowers are white and yellow.

Aphyllanthes [Liliaceae]

On hot hills in Mediterranean regions you may see rush-like tufts of narrow leaves which will not inspire you until you see the gentian-blue flower which ends each stem. *A. monspeliensis* is the only species in this genus and demands a hot, dry, sunny position.

Aquilegia [Ranunculaceae]
These popular and decorative plants are distributed far and wide over the Northern Hemisphere. The great problem with the whole family is its almost total lack of morals. Nearly all of them will hybridise with any other within bee-range or wind-range and, as the only satisfactory method of propagation is by means of seeds, the uncertainty of their progeny is exasperating.
— *alpina* from the Alps, with its lovely blue and white flowers, is seldom seen true in gardens.
— *bertolonii* is a 4-in pygmy which very often breeds true. Each stem carries one surprisingly large rich blue flower.
— *discolor* is another dwarf and also less willing to hybridise than most and displays blue and cream flowers above finely cut leaves.
— *jonesii* from the north-west of America is one of the most aggravating of the genus. From its small tufts of grey leaves should emerge 3 in stems carrying a large blue flower, but it is curiously reluctant to flower with any freedom.
— *saximontana* and *scopulorum* are both Americans and are more generous. Quite dwarf, they offer blue flowers and blue and white flowers with comparative freedom.

Arabis [Cruciferae]
There are weeds and treasures in this large genus.
— *albida* is the common white arabis, now more correctly named *A. caucasica*. Like *Alyssum* and *Aubrieta*, and any of its forms, it occupies a good deal of space and has only a brief floral display. Choose one of its several named clones.
— *blepharophylla* is a short-lived but pretty little American and is one of the earliest spring flowers. From its tufts of stiff leaves emerge heads of flowers which may be white, pink or rose-purple.
— *bryoides* is a cushion plant for the alpine-house or a choice nook in a sink or trough garden. It forms packed mounds of grey-haired tiny leaves and its white flowers are borne on 1 in-high stems. Give it the same treatment accorded to the rarer androsaces.

Arcterica [Ericaceae]
There is only one species, *A. nana*, from mountain woodlands in Japan. It is not difficult if you can provide it with a cool position and acid soil. An ideal peat-garden plant, it threads its way about, forming modest mats of tiny, glossy evergreen leaves. The urn-

shaped cream flowers are seen in little terminal clusters in late spring.

Arenaria [Caryophyllaceae]
This genus is closely related to *Alsine* and *Minuartia*, with which there is considerable confusion.
— *balearica* has no height at all. It loves to spread over the face of moist rocks or bricks where it becomes a green film, studded with myriads of tiny white flowers, all dancing on frail 1 in-high stems. It is easy to care for in the right place.
— *caespitosa* see *Sagina*.
— *ledebouriana* is a splendid crevice plant. From stony nooks it foams out in a cataract of narrow, grey-green leaves and sprays of good white flowers.
— *purpurascens* from the Pyrenees, abandons the family tradition of bearing white flowers and studs its prostrate mats of green leaves with soft lavender-purple flowers.
— *tetraquetra* comes from the high Sierras of Spain and is a cushion plant of a quality equalling any treasured alpine-house plant. Its wee leaves of grey-green are arranged four-angled on the short stems and compressed into dense pads, sometimes adorned by stemless white flowers. It has a form, 'Granatensis', which is even more densely compact.

Arisarum [Araceae]
This odd little aroid, *A. proboscideum*, must be grown if you have children. Give it a cool position in almost any soil and, from its slightly tuberous roots, it throws up bright green leaves. In early spring it would appear that a host of long-tailed mice were plunging head first into the foliage, for the olive-green and white flowers have long 'tails'.

Armeria [Plumbaginaceae]
These are the thrifts.
— *caespitosa* (=*juniperifolia*) is a Spaniard. Its tight hummocks and mounds of narrow, dark-green leaves are freely starred by stemless tufts of pink flowers. It also has an improved form, known as 'Bevan's Variety', and there is a hybrid, named 'Beechwood', which is a little taller and deep pink. There is also a quite pleasant albino.
— *corsica* is no more than another variation on the theme of *A. maritima*, with flowers of a distinctive shade of brick-red.
— *maritima* is the wild sea pink, which stains with colour the headlands of the western coasts of the British Isles. In gardens we grow selected forms, such as 'Laucheana' and 'Vindictive', whose flowers are of particular richness and brilliance.

Arnica [Compositae]

From the lime-free sub-alpine meadows in Europe hails *A. montana*. Its rosettes of quite large, softly hairy leaves emit tall stems bearing large flowers with rays of richest yellow.

Artemisia [Compositae]

This is a race of sometimes aromatic, usually silver-leaved, occasionally shrubby, sun-loving plants which, with one or two exceptions, are easy to cultivate. Mat-forming, or erect-stemmed, with grey or silver foliage and flowers of small importance, it is by their foliage that they attract admiration. Any of the following fulfil the above qualifications: *A. assoana, A. lanata, A. schmidtiana* 'Nana'. *A. glacialis* and *A. mutellina* are European high alpines which are not easy but may be persuaded by a sunny, gritty scree to display their splendid mats of argent foliage. *A. stelleriana* is a coarseness not to be placed near less vigorous plants, but it grows into magnificent mounds of silver foliage and is splendid on a wall.

Asarina [Scrophulariaceae]

A trailer with a liking for a cool position, *A. procumbens* has slightly sticky stems set with hairy, grey-green leaves. The large flowers are white, but tinted with yellow and pink. It flowers spasmodically throughout the summer.

Asperula [Rubiaceae]

— *lilaciflora* 'Caespitosa' should be grown in a sunny place and in very gritty soil. It presents a colourful prostrate mat of rich pink flowers.

— *odorata* is a pretty wanderer for shady places and is native to the British Isles. It is more correctly known as *Galium odoratum*. The stems and leaves can be dried and enclosed in muslin bags. Placed among linen they impart a pleasant fragrance.

— *suberosa* from Greece is delectable but slightly temperamental. It resents winter wet on its carpets of intensely soft and hairy leaves, which it conceals, when happy, beneath axillary clusters of tubular pink blossoms.

Aster [Compositae]

There are very few of this enormous genus which are truly appropriate to rock gardens.

— *alpinus* is a typical inhabitant of alpine meadows and is a good garden plant. The tufts of narrow leaves form the base for erect 9 in stems, each one carrying a large, purple-rayed and golden-centred aster flower. There is also a good albino with pure white flowers.

— *natalensis* comes from the Drakensburg Mountains of South Africa; it is hardy and very desirable. It roams modestly, emitting tufts of grey-green hairy leaves and 6 in stems carrying golden-eyed, gentian-blue, daisy-shaped flowers. Give it a sunny, warm situation.

Astilbe [Saxifragaceae]

Nearly all *Astilbe* are regarded as plants for the border and the sides of pools, ponds and streams, but there are just a few which are dainty miniatures, well fitted for a cool position in the rock garden, or in a peat garden. *Astilbe crispa* includes several well known named cultivars such as 'Gnome', 'Perkeo' and 'Kobald'. These make rosettes of crimped and crinkled leaves from which rise short spires of flowers, ranging in colour from white to pale and deep pink.

— *glaberrima* is the exquisite little Japanese species which is more correctly known as *A. japonica* 'Terrestris'. It has neat tufts of dark-green, sometimes bronzed, finely dissected leaves and graceful sprays of small pink flowers.

— *simplicifolia* is another Japanese, but the true species has been replaced in gardens by several so-called 'forms', which may be hybrids. *A. s.* 'Rosea' is one of the best. Rather taller than *A. glaberrima* it is otherwise similar, with loose sprays of rich pink flowers, carried over daintily cut foliage.

Aubrieta [Cruciferae]

These colourful commoners are always in great demand. There are wild species of *Aubrieta*, but these seldom wander outside the gates of botanic gardens. In gardens we grow an extensive range of named cultivars and any good alpine plant catalogue will present you with a score of names and colours from which to choose. These named kinds are all vegetatively propagated. If you sow any of the advertised strains of seeds you will end up with a mixture of colours, which is not helpful if you are planning a colour scheme. They all love sun and lime and they benefit from a fairly close hair-cut after flowering. Cuttings, made from the young, soft shoots which rise after such a trimming, root easily in sand.

Bellidiastrum [Compositae]

A not very distinguished plant, *B. michelii* inhabits alpine meadows in Europe. Its enlarged daisy flowers are white, sometimes just flushed with pink.

Bellis [Compositae]

There are other and more appropriate places for double daisies than in rock gardens. There are two, however, which I welcome.

— *rotundifolia* 'Caerulescens' comes from North Africa and is like the common lawn daisy but soft blue in colour.

— *sylvestris* comes from Southern France and this, too, resembles the common daisy, but its large flowers have the tips of the white ray florets strongly marked with crimson.

Betula [Betulaceae]

A truly miniature dwarf birch tree, *B. nana* is a rare native of the British Isles. It makes a sprawling bush of woody stems and is one of the more desirable dwarf rock garden shrubs.

Boykinia [Saxifragaceae]

The classical home of *B. jamesii* is Pike's Peak in Colorada, USA. It is rare in cultivation. Its thick leaves are coarsely toothed and grow in tight tufts from which rise 6–9 in stems bearing racemes of carmine-crimson flowers in summer. To ensure flowering, a measure of austerity is desirable. Under soft conditions in rich soil it tends to produce leaves rather than flowers.

Calamintha [Labiatae]

— *alpina* is a neat and easy little plant which makes loose tufts, less than 6 in high, and, in summer, carries on its branching stems whorls of purple flowers.

— *grandiflora* is similar, but a little larger in all its parts. Its flowers have a hint of red in the purple colour.

Calceolaria [Scrophulariaceae]

Few members of this large family qualify as rock garden plants.

— *biflora* is like most calceolarias in hailing from South America. It makes a pleasant show in a cool position where it will display its pouched yellow flowers on 1 ft-high stems.

— *darwinii* and *fothergillii* are both from wind-swept areas in the Straits of Magellan, Patagonia and the Falkland Islands and are the two star-turns. The tufts of toothed, dark green leaves of *C. darwinii* are smooth and those of *C. fothergillii* softly hairy. They both produce astonishing flowers of yellowish brown with a bar of startling white across the pouch. Curiously, considering their natural habitat, in gardens they prefer a position sheltered from cold winds and a gritty soil, rich in humus. Hardy enough to be grown in the open, they are more often given alpine-house treatment. There are now some amusing hybrids being raised between the two species.

— *tenella* comes from Chile and is quite prostrate, its frail stems rooting as they grow. On 2 in stems over the mats of soft green leaves are several small, pouched yellow flowers.

Campanula [Campanulaceae]

This genus of plants is of great importance to alpine gardeners. Most flower during the summer, after the first flush of spring blossom is over, and they are invaluable for continuing the display of colour. In general, they are easily grown in any good garden soil but exceptions will be noted.

— *alpestris* (= *allionii*) is from high European screes and should be given very gritty soil and perfect drainage. It spreads modestly by underground stolons emitting, here and there, tufts of narrow leaves. From such tufts, spring several short stems carrying large, purple-blue flowers.

— *arvatica* is a Spaniard and also asks for gritty, rather austere growing conditions. Its mats of tiny, sometimes notched, leaves form a carpet from which spring 3 in stems carrying a few star-shaped blossoms of violet-blue. It has also produced a desirable albino with pure white flowers.

— *barbata* is the bearded bell-flower of European and Scandinavian mountains. It is not long-lived, but provides plenty of seed from which it is easily increased. From a long tap-root emerge roughly hairy leaves and erect, 1 ft-high stems carrying many pendant blue bells, hairy on the inside. White-flowered forms are commonly produced among the seedlings. 4

— *betulifolia* is a beautiful species from Armenia, worthy of a place in the alpine-house, although hardy and handsome in a stone trough or emerging from a rocky crevice. Its semi-procumbent leafy stems end in loose clusters of bell-flowers, varying in colour from almost white to soft pink. Even before the flowers expand it is attractive as the buds are wine-red in colour. 5

— *carpatica* is now really an umbrella name for the numerous forms, hybrids and selections. The type is seldom seen outside botanical collections. Originally from the Carpathians, and known in gardens since the end of the eighteenth century, it is a race of easily grown and highly decorative plants demanding no special care or attention. The large flowers of open bell-shape are boldly displayed on erect stems, the colour ranging from white, through various blues, to deep purple-blue, according to the particular named clone or form. The height varies from 6 in to 1 ft, again according to form, and any alpine plant catalogue will offer a selection from which to choose.

— *cenisia* haunts the high places of European mountains and offers a challenge to those who try to please it. It is a lime-hater and grows naturally in almost pure grit. Try it in shallow pans in the alpine-house; keep it fairly dry during the winter but water freely in the spring and, if you are clever or lucky, enjoy its funnel-shaped, grey-blue flowers borne on very short stems.

— *cochlearifolia* (=*pusilla*) is an absolute necessity. By means of thread-fine roots it spreads below ground, erupting in tiny tufts of wee, glossy green leaves and, on 3 in stems, hanging its small bells of lavender or blue or white.

— *excisa* is a pretty, dwarf species and, given lime-free soil, should grow without difficulty. Its thin, erect 3–4 in stems each carry one slightly pendant blue flower. To keep it happy, divide it frequently and replant in fresh soil.

— *formaneckiana* is an extremely handsome monocarpic species from Macedonia. It makes a magnificent alpine-house specimen, with a bold rosette of crinkled grey leaves from which rises an erect, leafy stem. From every leaf axil springs a large tubular flower. The colour is usually white, but some seedlings produce bells finished with blue or pink.

— *garganica* is another variable species of which several named clones are grown. They are all splendid wall and crevice plants, their stems radiating and clinging closely to any adjacent rock or stone surface. The star-shaped flowers are produced in abundance on long trails and, according to the particular named form, may be white, soft or deep blue, or blue and white.

— 'G. F. Wilson' is a handsome

hybrid between *C. pulla* and *C. carpatica* and retains its vigour, whereas many fine old garden hybrids have become exhausted with age and are disappearing. Over the neat tufts of leaves, sometimes slightly yellow-green in colour, are large bell-flowers of purple blue.

— *herzegovensis* is a miniature and seen in its most desirable form as *C. h.* 'Nana', a version discovered by my late father. It asks for a rocky crevice and gritty soil, or a stony scree, and grows as a 1 in-high tuft of dark green leaves from which rise short stems in profusion carrying starry deep blue flowers. **6**

— *morettiana* is a saxatile haunter of narrow crevices in dolomitic cliffs. It should be wedged between small stones in pots or pans. The small, ivy-shaped leaves make little tufts from which emerge the 1 in-high stems, each carrying one large open bell of violet-blue.

·— *persicifolia* is the tall bell-flower of herbaceous borders, but it has a curious microform, *C. nitida* (=*planiflora*), which has tiny huddled rosettes of crinkled dark leaves and short, erect stems bearing blue or white wide open bells. It must be propagated vegetatively. If seeds are sown they produce only typical tall *C. persicifolia*.

— *portenschlagiana* (=*muralis*) is a popular, easily grown and beautiful plant. It will flourish in sun or light shade, in walls or in the rock garden or as an edging to a border. Its leafy mats disappear beneath the innumerable panicles of blue flowers.

— *poscharskyana* is a rumbustious ramper ideal for quickly clothing areas where little else will grow. It flourishes in the poorest of soil and is splendid in a wall. It creates a widespread entanglement of leafy stems which carry innumerable axillary clusters of lavender-blue flowers. 7

— *pulla* is from the Eastern Alps and on its 4 in stems carries many pendulous blossoms of luminous purple. *C.* × *pulloides* is a hybrid between this species and *C. carpatica*. It has slightly larger flowers of a lighter blue colour on 6 in stems.

— *raddeana* comes from Trans-Caucasica. It runs about—mildly, and forms colonies of tufted, glossy triangular leaves and the branching 1 ft-high stems bear showers of violet-blue flowers.

— × *rotarvatica* is a natural hybrid between *C. arvatica* and the British harebell, *C. rotundifolia*. It is an equable plant, inheriting the easy constitution of one parent, and carrying, on 4–6 in stems, the bright blue flowers of the other.

— *sarmatica* is another Caucasian and makes hummocks of grey, crinkled leaves; on 1 ft-high stems, it displays one-sided racemes of

pendant light blue bells. Easily raised from seed, it will usually present you with a few pleasing albinos.

— *thyrsoides* is exceptional in this genus in having blossoms of straw-yellow; they are strongly fragrant and carried on a stout, erect spike about 1 ft in height. It is monocarpic, but easily raised from seed.

— *zoysii* comes from the Eastern Alps and is one of the treasures of the genus. It is not all that difficult to grow, but is the most favoured diet of any slug in its vicinity. It likes limy, gritty soil with plenty of humus. The tiny, glossy leaves make wee tufts at ground level and the short stems bear clear blue flowers of curious shape, the mouth of the bell being crimped and puckered.

Cardamine [Cruciferae]

— *pratensis* is the common cuckoo flower of British meadows and, although a pretty plant, is not to be trusted in the garden. There is, however, a form with fully double lavender-pink flowers which is well behaved and a pleasant occupant of a cool corner.

— *trifolia* is very different. It comes from the Alps of Europe and makes little hummocks of trifoliate leaves; the heads of small white flowers are carried on 4–6 in stems.

42

Cassiope [Ericaceae]

If you can provide lime-free soil or a peat bed in a cool, lightly shaded position, then you must grow *Cassiope*. There are several species and hybrids from which to choose. They vary in the height of their stems, which are always clothed in evergreen, scale-like leaves, from the low mats of *C. lycopodioides* to the erect, 1 ft-high stems of *C. fastigiata* and *C. mertensiana*. They come from many regions in the Northern Hemisphere and their common feature is the white or cream, urn-shaped bells, which peep from between the scaly leaves which envelop the stems so closely. There exist a dozen or so others, often offered in the catalogues of specialist growers.

Catananche [Compositae]

A rarity recently re-introduced from the Atlas Mountains of North Africa, *C. caespitosa* has rosettes of narrow grey leaves, which emit branching stems carrying soft yellow flowers. Treasure it in the alpine-house and water only moderately during the winter. **8**

Centaurium [Gentianaceae]

A pleasant little plant, *C. scilloides* (=*portense*, =*Erythraea diffusa* =*E. massoni*) carries clear pink flowers, rather like those of a small gentian in shape, on short stems in spring and summer.

Cerastium [Caryophyllaceae]

Never allow the common snow in summer, *C. tomentosum*, to invade your rock garden. If left to colonise, nothing short of total rebuilding will eradicate it. *C. lanatum* is safer, making mats of grey-haired leaves and proving a useful carpeter with quite pretty white flowers.

Chamaecyparis [Cupressaceae]

Of the conifers, only a few of the most desirable pygmies have been included. Amongst the forms of *C. obtusa* are to be found some excellent, very slow-growing, bun-shaped conifers ideal for rock gardens and even for stone sinks and troughs. **9**

Cheiranthus [Cruciferae]

The old double Scotch wallflower, *C. cheiri* 'Harpur Crewe' is by no means an alpine plant, but its rigid bushes, up to 18 in in height, make excellent dwarf shrubs and are smothered for weeks on end in clusters of fully double, yellow, strongly fragrant flowers. It makes too few roots to adequately support its bushy top growth and may need a little support. In the event of a mishap it is easily increased from cuttings.

Chiastophyllum [Crassulaceae]

The charming little *C. oppositifolium* (= *Cotyledon oppositifolia*) inhabits narrow chinks and crannies in walls and between rocks, from which it hangs out slender chains of golden flowers, for all the world like those of a baby laburnum. Its only demand is a cool position.

Chrysanthemum [Compositae]

Very few chrysanthemums qualify as rock garden plants, and some of those have now been moved into different genera, e.g. *Leucanthemum*, *Tanacetum* and *Pyrethrum*.
— *alpinum* is a neat little European alpine making tiny tufts of deeply cut, greyish leaves which it adorns in summer with surprisingly large white, golden-eyed flowers. It is at its best in a very sunny, gritty scree and even there may not be very long-lived, but it can be raised from seed.
— *haradjanii* see *Tanacetum*.

Chrysogonum [Compositae]

The only species in this genus is *C. virginianum*, a North American plant of some virtue. Its procumbent and leafy stems spread out in dense carpets and are decorated in May and June with bright yellow flowers. It prefers a position that is not sun-baked.

Codonopsis [Campanulaceae]

A small genus, most of its members are from the Orient. They have fleshy, slightly tuberous roots and will mostly, given the opportunity, scramble upward through adjacent plants, which offer them

support. They prefer a light, well drained soil and a sunny position.
— *clematidea* has bells of light blue, pencilled inside with deeper colour.
— *convolvulacea* is one of the beauties of the race and deserves alpine-house treatment. It needs a few twigs to support the slender stems which carry large, rich blue flowers of open bell-shape.
— *meleagris* has large flowers, shaded green and yellow with chocolate lines marking the inside of the bells.
— *ovata* is the species most commonly grown and the interiors of its pale blue bells are decorated with purple veins and a basal dark blotch outlined in green.

Conandron [Gesneriaceae]

The only species in this genus, *C. ramondioides*, hails from Japan. It enjoys a cool crevice or a position in the peat garden. The large, deeply crinkled green leaves form a handsome setting for the cymes of lilac-purple, orange-centred flowers. Increase it by means of seeds, division or, with care, leaf cuttings.

Cornus [Cornaceae]

A creeping shrub most suitable for lime-free soil, *C. canadensis* (= *Chamaepericlymenum canadense*) is a good ground-coverer. It grows thick mats of leathery leaves. The small flowers are surrounded by four showy pure white bracts and followed by bright red berries.

Cortusa [Primulaceae]

A small cousin of the primulas, *C. matthioli* inhabits mountain woodlands in Europe and Asia. Over its tufts of hairy, heart-shaped leaves are 6 in stems bearing one-sided clusters of pendant pink flowers during the spring.

Cotula [Compositae]

These are frankly invasive, but, like *Acaena*, are useful as carpeters in sunny positions, or as inhabitants of chinks between paving-stones. Their flowers have little value, but the foliage is attractive and any of the following will be found useful and pleasing: *C. potentillina*, *C. reptans* and *C. squalida*. They are all natives of Australasia.

Crassula [Crassulaceae]

This is a large family of South African, mostly non-hardy plants. — *sarcocaulis* is hardy in an alpine-house and makes a fascinating dwarf, gnarled tree, its shoots ending in clusters of crimson buds which open into pink flowers.

— *sedifolia* is hardy, except in exceptionally wet and cold winters, and makes congested pads of crowded rosettes of tiny leaves, studded with heads of small white flowers. A good cushion plant, it is quite suitable for stone sinks and troughs.

Crepis [Compositae]

Only two of these are likely to tempt alpine gardeners. Both are sun-lovers, flourish in any good soil and can be propagated from seed.

— *aurea*, when not in flower, closely resembles a dandelion, but the scene changes when it carries its bronze-orange flowers in summer.

— *incana* is more of an aristocrat, making hummocks of stiff, branching stems clothed in narrow, notched grey leaves and displaying myriads of pink composite flowers.

Cyananthus [Campanulaceae]

This small but exquisite genus of *Campanula* cousins comes from Asia. Given open, sunny positions and soil which is essentially sharply drained and, at the same time, not lacking in humus, they will grow very contentedly. They have a prostrate, spreading habit and flower from early summer onward. Propagate by seeds and cuttings—they do not divide readily, as they mostly grow from a single tap root.

— *lobatus* is one of the best. From the apex of its thick root radiate leafy stems, each of which terminates in a wide open, rounded flower of blue, rivalling a gentian blossom in intensity. There is also an albino with pure white blossoms.

— *microphyllus* (= *incanus*) is a smaller plant, with tiny leaves but a similar habit of growth and the rich blue flowers are rather more funnel-shaped.

— *sherriffii* has some right to be regarded as the supreme cyananthus. It comes from the heights of Tibet and forms dense tufts of stems and leaves clothed in silver-grey hairs. The large, slightly tubular flowers of clear, light blue are prettily bearded in the throat —as, indeed, are the blossoms of other species. It merits, and appreciates, alpine-house treatment.

Cyclamen [Primulaceae]

This is another important genus. All the species grow from tuberous roots and it is important to obtain them when they are actually in growth, or are at least freshly lifted from stock beds, even if they are dormant. Dried tubers are often offered for sale, but these may take some years to develop as they form a hard and corky 'skin' when exposed to the air for long periods. Some are completely hardy, others need slight winter protection. They all have a period of dormancy, which varies according to their particular flowering period. The following are likely to be readily available and the first three described would

make a splendid trinity with which to begin.

— *hederifolium* (= *neapolitanum*) is the most widely grown and deservedly popular of them all and offers its pink or white flowers in the autumn. The leaves which follow the flowers are extremely decorative, being marbled and patterned in green and white.

— *purpurascens* (= *europaeum*) is summer-flowering and its carmine flowers are sweetly fragrant.

— *repandum* fills the mountain woodlands of Corsica and Sardinia with beauty in the early spring. The carmine-red flowers have long, slightly twisted petals and are often fragrant. It, too, has a charming albino. It is not as absolutely hardy as the other two, but will succeed outside in sheltered corners.

— *coum* must be regarded as an umbrella name covering a widely variable group of delightful plants. Widely distributed throughout Europe, Asia Minor and the Caucasus, it has developed into many geographic forms. The leaves may be round or kidney-shaped, they may be entirely green or marked with silver lines. The flowers have short petals which may be near-white, pink or deep crimson.

— *graecum* is also an extremely variable plant. It inhabits warm Mediterranean regions and is not reliably hardy but is a magnificent alpine-house plant. The flowers are coloured soft rose-pink and the petals are marked at the base with two purple blotches. It is the foliage, however, which is most exciting. Infinitely variable in the patterning of silver on the deep-green base colour, no two plants are precisely similar.

— *persicum* is the species from which the large-flowered hybrid cyclamen originated and the wild forms, although not at all hardy, are graceful and elegant plants for a cold green-house. It, too, is variable; the flowers may be pink, white or red and many are strongly fragrant.

Cymbalaria [Scrophulariaceae]

— *aequitriloba* is also known as Kenilworth ivy and is a charming little nuisance which spreads avidly. If confined to the chinks of a stony wall it is quite delightful, adorning its carpets of tiny, ivy-shaped leaves with countless small purple-pink flowers all summer.

— *hepaticifolia* is also a wanderer, but never to the point of being a pest; it threads its way about, erupting into ground-hugging groups of greyish, kidney-shaped leaves. The petals of the flowers are lavender-coloured, with dark tips.

Daphne [Thymeliaceae]

The dwarf species of *Daphne* are some of the most desirable rock garden shrubs, but they are temperamental. Try any of the following and do your best with them: *D. arbuscula*, *D. blagayana*, *D. cneorum*, *D. collina*, *D. retusa* and, gem of gems, *D. petraea*. All but the last named are outdoor plants, but *D. petraea*, a cliff-dweller, is usually given the distinction of alpine-house treatment. It is slow-growing but ultimately rewarding when smothered with the tubular, pink, intensely fragrant flowers.

Delphinium [Ranunculaceae]

One does not expect delphiniums to be rock garden plants, but there are a few dwarf species which qualify. The following two are most likely to be obtainable.

— *nudicaule* is a short-lived but lovely Californian with panicles of red or orange flowers on short stems in summer.

— *tatsienense* comes from China and is an elegant species, carrying its violet-blue flowers with tiny orange beards in loose corymbs on 1 ft-high stems. Increase them both from seeds and give them sunny positions in any good soil.

Dianthus [Caryophyllaceae]

With one or two exceptions, members of this genus are all lime-lovers and relish open, sunny places. Some of the best species and a few of the hybrids and named forms are described.

— *alpinus* grows as prostrate pads

of narrow green leaves and its large, and beautifully rounded flowers, with overlapping petals of rich rose-crimson, stud the mats on 2 in stems. It likes lime and leafy, gritty soil. It is sometimes attacked by the carnation fly, *Hylomya brunnescens*. Any good soil insecticide should control the problem. Take great care in following the instructions on the container.

— *arvernensis* has a mysterious provenance. My own thought is that it must have been derived from wild *D. gratianopolitanus* (= *caesius*). It is a splendid mat of grey foliage studded by innumerable rich pink flowers on short stems—and it has an equally attractive albino.

— *callizonus* is like *D. alpinus* in habit, but the equally large flowers are lavender-pink with a flecked white central zone.

— *carthusianorum* is not one of the most beautiful *Dianthus*, but has survived in gardens for more than four hundred years, so it must have some appeal! Its magenta flowers are carried in clusters atop stems which may be more than 1 ft in height.

— *deltoides* is the maiden pink and a British native. A very variable plant, its flowers may be white, pink or red. It should be grown in one of its selected forms, which have dark-green foliage and flowers of especially brilliant colour, e.g. 'Flashing Lights', 'Wisley Variety' and 'Bowles's Variety'.

— *graniticus* is an exception which likes lime-free soil. It resembles *D. deltoides* in some ways, but is dwarfer, with clusters of small but bright pink flowers.

— *gratianopolitanus* (= *caesius*) is the Cheddar pink, now a rarity in the Cheddar Gorge, British Isles, where it should be left unmolested. It is grown as one of the many selected and named forms, and many garden hybrids claim it as one of their parents. In general, the forms make mats and cushions of narrow grey leaves and adorn them with flowers in various shades of pink.

— *haematocalyx* is a gem from Greece. Its hard, narrow, pointed grey leaves form tight cushions on which rest short-stemmed flowers of purple-red, the petals painted cinnamon-yellow on the reverse. An especially neat and compact form exists under the name of *D. h.* 'Alpinus'. 11

— *knappii* departs from the family tradition and carries clear yellow flowers. It comes from Eastern Europe and is of an untidy, straggling habit, but the flowers are very attractive and, if it is grown in association with other plants, its rather gawky stems are unobserved.

— *microlepis* is a Bulgarian and another of the few which prefer lime-free soil. The neat, circular pads of grey leaves form a good setting for the clear pink, short-stemmed flowers. *D. musalae*, also from Bulgaria, is of similar habit but the flowers are glowing red in colour. Both species ask for gritty scree conditions or alpine-house treatment.

— *myrtinervis* is really a microform of *D. deltoides* which has achieved specific rank. It makes the flattest of flat mats of tiny leaves, which it jewels with stemless bright pink flowers. To retain the desirable tight habit, it should be treated with some austerity and given very gritty soil.

— *noeanus* has very narrow, almost spiky foliage and the fragrant white flowers are borne in showers on 9 in stems.

— *pavonius* (= *neglectus*) is a lime-hater and a lovely dianthus. The thin leaves make dense cushions, from which rise the short stems bearing large pale or deep pink flowers, but always with a strong wash of buff-colour on the reverse of the petals.

— *squarrosus* comes from the USSR and has slightly spiny leaves and, on 9 in stems, bears white flowers whose petals are deeply fringed and sweetly fragrant.

— *strictus* 'Brachyanthus' is a very charming miniature with pads of grey leaves and rather long, lax stems carrying small but shapely flowers which may be white or pink. 12

— *superbus* has been known in gardens since the thirteenth century. It is untidy but that is a fault that is readily forgiven when it covers its sprawling mats of wide leaves with branching stems carrying many fragrant, lavender-pink, green-eyed flowers with petals deeply slashed in fine segments.

Diascia [Scrophulariaceae]

Not many South African plants are hardy, but *D. cordata*, from the Drakensburg Mountains, is hardy and invaluable. The semi-prostrate stems bear short racemes of pretty terracotta-pink flowers throughout the summer. Give it a warm and sunny spot in any good garden soil.

Dicentra [Papaveraceae]

Most of the few species of *Dicentra* are too tall for rock gardens, but the exceptions are *D. canadensis* and *D. cucullaria*, both from North America. From tiny tubers spring deeply cut grey-green leaves and short racemes of lyre-shaped flowers. The flowers of *D. canadensis* are white; those of *D. cucullaria* are also white, but yellow-tipped. *D. peregrina*, from Japan, has never really settled down in British gardens. Its dissected grey-green leaves and elegant pink flowers are truly exciting, but it needs great care and alpine-house conditions.

Dionysia [Primulaceae]
All the members of this enticing and exciting genus, which is as captivating as the Aretian androsaces, come from the Middle East and the Southern USSR. Of the forty or so known species, a few are in cultivation. The one which has shown the greatest adaptability is *D. aretioides*, which builds up domed cushions of closely packed rosettes of tiny, hairy, grey-green leaves. The whole plant disappears in the spring beneath countless stemless, primrose-scented yellow flowers. In nature dionysias are subjected to long dry periods and so must be watered with the utmost care during their resting periods. Other species which are occasionally available are *D. bryoides* (pink flowers), *D. curviflora* (lavender-pink flowers) and *D. tapetodes* (long-tubed and yellow flowers).

Dodecatheon [Primulaceae]
All the species are native to North America and, of the several in cultivation, *D. meadia* is the most common. On tallish stems it carries umbels of pink flowers, the petals sharply reflexed. They all like a cool position in moist soil and are frequently grown with candelabra primulas.

Doronicum [Compositae]
A delightful, early-flowering dwarf plant, *D. cordatum* likes sun and any good soil. From clumps of heart-shaped leaves rise short stems bearing large golden-rayed flowers.

Douglasia [Primulaceae]
— *laevigata* is North American and to be admired for its neat tufts of green, rosetted leaves and heads of rose-red flowers, carried on 2–3 in stems in spring. Without being too intolerant, it prefers lime-free soil.

— *vitaliana* is a European alpine and makes mats of ash-grey leaves which it obscures beneath a wealth of fragrant yellow flowers. The variety *D. v.* ssp. *praetutiana* is more silvery in leaf and even more free-flowering.

Draba [Cruciferae]
— *aizoides* is a pretty commoner with rosettes of small, rigid leaves and 2 in stems carrying small heads of yellow flowers. It is not sensational but is well worth growing.

— *bryoides* from the Caucasus is an aristocrat and makes soft, rounded cushions of tiny green leaves and offers its small, bright golden flowers in clusters at the top of thread-fine 1 in-high stems in early spring.

— *dedeana* comes from Spain and gathers its stiff, bristle-tipped leaves into rosettes from which rise short stems carrying crowded heads of white flowers.

— *mollissima* is a Caucasian and qualifies for the alpine-house. Its domes of closely packed soft green leaves are hidden in spring beneath many small heads of yellow flowers. Give it very gritty soil and water it with discretion in the winter.

— *polytricha* comes from Eastern Europe and packs its small, grey-green leaves into dense domes which hide beneath the array of golden flowers in spring. Again this is a plant for the alpine-house and discreet watering.

Dryas [Rosaceae]

— *octopetala* is more commonly known as the mountain avens and is widely distributed in Europe and the British Isles. Its woody stems spread at ground level, clad with small, leathery, oak-like leaves. The large saucer-shaped, eight-petalled flowers are borne on short stems in spring and summer.

— *drummondii* is its American cousin, similar in leaf and habit but with yellow flowers that seldom expand fully.

— *suendermannii* is a hybrid between the two which expands its buds into cream-coloured flowers.

Edraianthus [Campanulaceae]

This genus is often confused with *Wahlenbergia*, although a simple distinction, covering most instances, is that the flowers of *Edraianthus* are carried in clusters and those of *Wahlenbergia* singly. Mostly from warm and sunny areas in Eastern Europe, there is so much similarity between such species as *E. caudatus*, *E. graminifolius*, *E. kitaibelii* and *E. serbicus* that, beyond stating that it is their habit to form low, twiggy bushlets of woody stems and to carry blue, or purple-blue flowers in clusters during the summer, I shall comment only on one of the gems of the race, *E. pumilio*. This is a miniature, and excellent for planting in a stone trough or sink, or in a sunny, gritty scree. Its neat and tidy tufts of narrow, greyish leaves form a cushion upon which rest the funnel-shaped flowers of violet-blue. They can all be propagated by cuttings or seeds. 14

Epigaea [Ericaceae]

These are very definitely plants for cool and lime-free conditions. A peat bed provides their ideal home. They flower in the spring and early summer and can be increased from seed, or by very careful division of old plants, but they invariably sulk after being uprooted and will take some time to settle down.

— *asiatica* is Japanese with prostrate, hairy, woody stems, which will root as they spread, forming low mats of rounded, leathery leaves. The white, or pink, bell-shaped flowers are slightly fragrant.

—*gaultherioides* (= *Orphanidesia*) is a great rarity from the neighbourhood of the Black Sea. In cultivation, it demands almost total shade. Similar in habit to the preceding species, it carries short racemes of large, cup-shaped soft pink flowers in the leaf axils. It is a very beautiful plant, difficult to obtain and difficult to grow, but worth any effort.

—*repens* comes from North America and is reasonably amenable. Its small flowers are urn-shaped and white or soft pink.

Erigeron [Compositae]

A huge genus, distributed far and wide over the temperate world, this contains few kinds really appropriate for rock gardens. Of these, one or two are very desirable. They are all sun-lovers and not at all difficult to grow. Propagation is by seed or division.

—*aurantiacus* is from Turkestan and may be a trifle large, but its bright orange flower heads on 1 ft-high stems are decorative.

— *aureus* is an alpine treasure from North America. From neat humps of grey-haired leaves rise very short stems, each carrying one large flower of richest gold. It is an ideal scree, trough or alpine-house plant and flowers continu-ously throughout the summer.

—*compositus* is a tiny American plant, with segmented leaves and flowers which are pale blue, or almost white.

—*flettii* is endemic to the Olympic Mountains of Washington, USA. Similar in habit to *E. aureus*, but a little larger, it has pure white flowers. A natural hybrid between the two species occurred in my nursery and has been named *E.* 'Birch Hybrid'. Its flowers are softly cream in colour.

— *mucronatus* is a delightful weed, now more correctly called *E. karvinskianus*. Mexican in origin, it has spread itself world-wide by means of its freely distributed seeds. Let it inhabit cracks and crannies in walls, or between paving-stones or stone steps. It will flower the summer through, its daisy flowers changing as they age from white to pink to deep rose-pink.

Erinacea [Leguminosae]

The only member in its genus, *E. anthyllis* (= *pungens*) is distributed from the Pyrenees to North Africa. Its stiff, spine-tipped stems grow into hard spiky, domed huddles. Clustered on the stems in late spring are violet-blue flowers. It is an avid sun-lover suited to hot, dry places or the alpine-house.

Erinus [Scrophulariaceae]

Of the few species, *E. alpinus* is the

only one of interest here. An easy free-seeder, but too pretty ever to be a nuisance, it joyfully inhabits chinks and crannies, where it makes neat tufts of tiny leaves which it shrouds with short-stemmed clusters of white, soft or deep pink flowers. It seldom exceeds a couple of inches in height. It is not an aristocrat but a necessity. 13

Eritrichium [Boraginaceae]
Justice demands that mention be made of *E. nanum*, even though it has stubbornly refused to bestow its exquisite beauty upon our gardens. The experts persist in attempts to grow it but success very seldom attends their efforts. Leave it to the enthusiasts to try, and visit it in its native alpine habitats to admire its cushions of hairy leaves, smothered with stemless, rounded flowers of the clearest imaginable blue.

Erodium [Geraniaceae]
This genus of easily grown sun-lovers contains a number of invaluable rock garden plants, some mat-forming, others making low, bushy plants. They flower over long periods from spring onward and can all be increased by seeds, cuttings or division.
— *chamaedrioides* (now correctly *E. reichardii*) spreads into neat, prostrate mats of dark foliage which it studs with white, pink-

veined flowers. It is more commonly grown in the form 'Roseum', whose flowers are wholly pink. There is also a version with semi-double flowers, but this often reverts to the single-flowered type.
— *chrysanthum* forms its filigree silver foliage into tufts and the 9 in flower stems bear heads of soft yellow flowers. The sexes are on separate plants, the flowers of the male form being less attractive, but, if seeds are required, both sexes must be present.
— *corsicum* inhabits the sea-washed rocks of Corsican and Sardinian shores and should be given rocky crevices to inhabit. The slightly scalloped leaves are felted with grey hairs and the pink flowers are veined with deeper colour.

Others worth acquiring are *E. absinthoides*, *E. guttatum*, *E. macradenum*, *E. supracanum* and *E. trichomanifolium*.

Erysimum [Cruciferae]
These wallflower cousins are often confused with *Cheiranthus*, to which genus they are closely related. There are some weedy members, but one or two make a useful contribution. They are easily grown in open sunny positions and in any good soil, and can be increased from seeds or cuttings.
— *alpinum* comes from as far north in Europe as Scandinavia and car-

53

ries fragrant yellow flowers on 6 in stems.

— *linifolium* is Spanish and carries racemes of lilac flowers on 12 in stems.

— *pulchellum* comes from Asia Minor and displays its mustard-yellow flowers in crowded heads on 12 in stems.

Euphorbia [Euphorbiaceae]

Scattered about the world are more than a thousand species of *Euphorbia*, but only a few qualify as rock garden plants.

— *cyparissias* can be an almost ineradicable weed which runs and seeds too freely. However, given an area to itself, it pleases with its short, leafy stems and heads of greenish-yellow flowers and bracts. The foliage often takes rich autumn tints.

— *myrsinites* is very different. Given a position from which it can trail its long stems, clothed in scale-like grey, fleshy leaves and ending in heads of yellow bracts, it is extremely decorative.

Euryops [Compositae]

The only species demanding inclusion, *E. acraeus* (= *evansii*), was introduced, not very long ago, from South Africa. It forms a rigid 15 in bush of woody stems dressed in silver, narrow leaves and offers, in summer, heads of bright yellow flowers. It is very hardy and, indeed, is happier in a sunny outdoor position than under glass. 15

Festuca [Gramineae]

The alpine grasses serve a useful purpose when tucked into odd chinks and corners in the rock garden. If given the freedom of rich soil they will be too vigorous and can swamp less lusty neighbours. Any of the following will please: *F. alpina*, *F. eskia*, *F. glacialis*, *F. ovina*, *F. punctoria* and *F. rubra*.

Frankenia [Frankeniaceae]

A British native, *F. laevis* has flat carpets of tiny green leaves, obscured in summer by myriads of flesh-pink flowers. *F. thymifolia* comes from Spain and is of similar habit but with flowers of deeper pink and softly grey-haired foliage.

Gentiana [Gentianaceae]

This is one of the most important alpine families. Their needs are various but, unless otherwise stated in the descriptions, it may be assumed that an open, sunny position in any good, well drained soil will suffice. Those having (NL) after the description are very definitely for totally lime-free soil.

— *acaulis* is really a group name for *G. angustifolia*, *G. clusii*, *G. dinarica*, and *G. kochiana*, among others. The plant, known for so long as *G. acaulis* in gardens, is of unknown provenance. They all have large trumpet-shaped flowers of glorious blue. The group as a whole is apt to be shy-flowering in some situations. There is no scientific or valid explanation for this and the only solution appears to be to move the plants to another position. It is not unknown for a move of only a few yards to achieve success.

— *asclepiadea* is the graceful willow gentian, and it likes a cool position in which to develop its tall, arching, leafy stems, from which dangle the clusters of blue flowers. There is also a good albino.

— *bavarica* belongs to a small group of species from the high European mountains and with it can be included *G. brachyphylla* and *G. imbricata*. They resemble tiny versions of *G. verna* and are rather intractable, although beautiful.

— *bellidifolia* hails from New Zealand, and departs from the family tradition of blue flowers by carrying blossoms of ivory white on its dark stems. It can be grouped with the rather similar *G. saxosa*, also from the Antipodes.

— *farreri* is one of the Asiatic, late summer and autumn-flowering gentians which demand lime-free soil, rich in humus. Its prostrate mats of crowded stems are adorned by flowers of luminous Cambridge blue. It has hybridised so freely with other members of its group that the true original species is now a rarity in gardens. (NL)

— *gracillipes* is a Chinese species which makes a central rosette of narrow leaves from which radiate semi-prostrate stems, each carrying one bell-shaped purple-blue flower from mid-summer onward. (NL)

— *lagodechiana* is now hopelessly confused in gardens with *G. septemfida*, to which it is closely akin. Its flowers, however, are borne singly on the stems, whereas in *G. septemfida* they are in clusters. It is a useful, summer-flowering plant but you must resign yourself to the fact that the plant you get will probably be a form of *G. septemfida*.

— *lutea* is the tall gentian of alpine meadows. Its stately stems can tower to a height of 3 ft and carry, in the upper leaf axils, clusters of straw yellow flowers. It is not a beauty but has considerable 'architectural' value.

— *pneumonanthe* is the bog gentian, now a rarity in the wild. It likes a cool rather moist situation and carries, on its 1 ft-high stems, blue, tubular flowers. It is more interesting than beautiful and is best admired, but not uprooted, in the wild.

— *pyrenaica* is rather a problem for it, too, seldom yields to our persuasions in gardens. In nature it tends to inhabit moist, peaty places, entangled with other alpine flowers. The mats of small leaves emit single stems which carry the flowers of deep violet-blue during May and June.

— *septemfida* might well be described as 'everyman's gentian', for it will grow in almost any soil or situation, forming robust clumps of 1 ft-high, leafy stems terminating in clusters of blue, trumpet-shaped flowers. It flowers in mid- to late summer and is a thoroughly useful and reliable garden plant.

— *sino-ornata* is the type species of the invaluable group of Asian autumn-flowering species and hybrids which includes *G. s.* var. *alba*. From the time of its first introduction from China, many years ago, it has proved a firm favourite, given the lime-free soil that it inexorably demands. Over carpets of narrow green leaves it bears the azure trumpets in bounteous profusion from late August on into the winter months. Plant it in March/ April and divide and replant it every two or three years. (NL) **17 18**

— *verna* is the well-beloved spring gentian, a rare native and widely distributed throughout Europe. Its neat tufts of glossy green leaves crowd into dense tufts and emit short-stemmed flowers of incomparable blue early in the spring. It is seen at its finest in the form 'Angulosa'. Give it gritty, humus-rich soil and full sun and raise a few seedlings now and then, for it can eventually flower itself into extinction.

Hybrid gentians of the Asian group
Of the many autumn-flowering, lime-hating Asian gentians, few of the original species are now available. Their place has been taken by a host of splendid natural hybrids, all mat-forming and all with flowers of a shade of rich blue. Amongst the best are 'Devonhall', 'Hexa-Farreri' 'Inverleith' **(16)**, 'Kidbrooke Seedling', 'Macaulayi', 'Midnight', 'Stevenagensis' and 'Vorna'. They should all be given the same treatment as *G. sino-ornata*.

Geranium [Geraniaceae]

No one should experience any difficulty in growing the dwarf hardy geraniums suitable for rock gardens—and there are several of them. Unless stated otherwise, those described below are sun-lovers and will flourish in any good soil. They can be propagated from seeds, by division, or by rooted layers.

— *argenteum* comes from the mountains of Central and Eastern Europe. Its silky-haired leaves are handsomely silvered and deeply cleft. On 4 in stems, it carries good pink flowers, the petals veined with deeper colour.

—*celticum* is no more than a form of the wild herb Robert, *G. robertianum*, according to the botanists, but the plant I grow and like under this name does not suggest any such relationship. It is a tiny perennial, with finely cut leaves and showers of starry white flowers throughout the summer. It likes a cool niche in a wall and seeds itself harmlessly.

—*cinereum* comes from the Pyrenees and decorates its tufts of segmented, grey-green leaves with cup-shaped flowers of rounded shape and deep pink colour. The petals are commonly veined with deeper colour. The subspecies *subcaulescens* is a glory on its own, with crimson, dark-eyed flowers, and there is a possible hybrid, named 'Ballerina' whose ash-grey foliage is a pretty setting for the flowers of clear soft pink. **19**

—*dalmaticum* is from Eastern Europe and is a friendly little cushioner, making low mats of glossy leaves which take on rich autumn tints. The round pink flowers face full front on their 4–5 in stems and make a fine summer display. There is also a pleasing albino.

—*farreri* is a Chinese species from high altitudes and a choice plant for a sunny scree or even the alpine-house. It is also small enough to be grown in a sink or trough. Tufts of a few leaves emit short stems on which are cup-

shaped pink flowers, each with a central cluster of dark anthers. **20**

—*pylzowianum* from Tibet, is a mild wanderer, spreading by long, thin roots on which are tiny nodules, from which spring tufts of tiny dissected leaves and pink flowers on 3 in stems.

—*renardii* was introduced from the Caucasus by my father. Its quite large rounded leaves are velvety in texture and the flowers are soft lavender in colour. It is handsome in foliage as well as flower.

—*sanguineum* is the 'Bloody Cranesbill' and is too large for most rock gardens. Its variety *lancastriense* is a prostrate miniature which adorns its mats of dark green leaves with salver-shaped salmon-pink flowers and blossoms throughout the summer.

—*tuberosum* from Southern Europe has large tubers, from which arise hairy 9 in stems bearing violet-purple flowers. After flowering, it quickly dies down and is not seen again until the following spring.

—*wallichianum* should be grown in the form named 'Buxton's Blue'. It is a sprawling spreader with a liking for light shade. Its long, leafy stems carry many saucer-shaped flowers of clear light blue with a white centre. **21**

Geum [Rosaceae]

—*montanum* is a desirable dwarf species from the European Alps.

The round, hairy leaves grow in tufts on stout rhizomes. On short stems are large, rich yellow flowers.

— *reptans* is a splendid plant, happier in lime-free soil. It prefers a stony diet and should not be fed on rich soil. From the rosettes of leaves spread long stolons, like strawberry runners, which have rosettes of leaves at the tip and root into the soil. Singly, on 6 in stems, are huge, rounded golden flowers, which are followed by heads of decorative, long-awned seeds. Both species are spring- and early summer-flowering and are best increased from seeds.

Globularia [Globulariaceae]

This is a genus of dwarf, woody, almost shrubby little plants from dry and sunny situations in the Alps. They are summer-flowering.

— *cordifolia* forms its woody stems into prostrate mats. The small, dark green leaves are notched at the tips and the globular heads of blue flowers are carried on very short stems.

— *meridionalis* (= *bellidifolia*) develops tangles of woody, prostrate stems and has round heads of richly blue flowers.

— *nudicaulis* provides heads of similar flowers, but on taller stems, rising to about 9 in. 22

— *repens* (= *nana*) is the smallest of all, growing into dense, compact mats of entwined stems,

clothed with the tiniest of leathery leaves and deep blue flower heads on 1 in stems.

— *trichosantha* notches its basal leaves with three terminal teeth and displays the bright blue flowers in large, round heads on 9 in stems. Globularias seldom provide cutting material but they can be carefully divided, or raised from seed.

Gypsophila [Caryophyllaceae]

Most of the gypsophilas seen on rock gardens are forms of *G. repens*, but there are one or two others.

— *aretioides*, from the Caucasus and Iran, is a cushion plant *par excellence*, crowding its minute leaves into iron-hard hummocks. The white flowers are seldom produced in abundance, but, when they do appear, sit stemlessly on the pads of foliage. It will grow outdoors but is more often treated as an alpine-house specimen.

— *cerastioides* from the Himalayas, is a looser, softer plant and displays loose sprays of white, pink-veined flowers on short stems throughout the summer.

— *repens* itself is seldom grown, but it has several very garden-worthy forms, all of trailing habit and excellent crevice and wall plants. *G. r.* 'Fratensis' is one of the neatest and dwarfest, with rich pink flowers, *G. r.* 'Letchworth Rose' is slightly larger, and soft pink. *G. r.* 'Monstrosa' is more robust and has grey foliage and pure white flowers. **23**

All kinds, except *G. aretioides*, are easily increased by cuttings of soft tips.

Haberlea [Gesneriaceae]

A small family, native to the Balkans, its members should be grown in cool, north-facing or shaded crevices between rocks, or in walls. They blossom in spring and early summer and can be propagated by careful division, by leaf cuttings, or from seeds. *H. rhodopensis* makes rosettes of dark-green, hairy leaves, not unlike those of *Ramonda*, and the slightly tubular flowers are carried in pendant umbels. Their colour is lavender-lilac and there is a fine albino named 'Virginalis'. Although *H. ferdinandi-coburgii* is usually listed as a species, it is probably only a form of *H. rhodopensis*, which it closely resembles, except that the flowers are larger, more open-mouthed and show freckles of gold in their throats.

Hacquetia [Umbelliferae]

A happy little harbinger of spring, *H. epipactis* (= *Dondia*) flowers with the first of the snowdrops. The cleft leaves make neat tufts on which to display heads of tiny golden flowers set on a platter of green leaves, or bracts. It likes a cool, slightly shaded position in any good soil.

Helianthemum [Cistaceae]

Few dwarf, shrubby plants make a braver display throughout the summer than the sun-loving helianthemums. Most of those commonly grown come under the banner name of *H. nummularium*, but are listed in most catalogues under their cultivar names. There are many from which to choose, with colours ranging from white, through shades of pink to deep wine-red and diversions into yellow and orange. They will grow in any good soil and benefit from being trimmed back when the first flush of flowers diminishes. Two species quite different in character are *H. alpestre* 'Serpyllifolium', a prostrate shrub of neat and tidy habit with golden flowers, and *H. lunulatum*, more upright, with myriads of yellow flowers on the 9 in grey-leaved bushes.

Helichrysum [Compositae]

This immense genus is scattered through the Old World, largely in South Africa and Australasia. Many of them are hardy and desirable rock garden plants; all are sun-lovers and not in any way difficult to grow. Some of the choicer species are usually harboured in the alpine-house.

— *bellidioides* is a useful carpeter

to use as ground cover for small bulbs in the rock garden, and it will also enjoy being tucked into cracks between paving stones. It has mats of grey leaves and white, 'everlasting' flowers on very short stems.

— *coralloides* is a fascinating plant of shrubby habit, its rigid branches set with scale-like leaves of green, showing round each one a margin of white 'wool'. It makes a small, gnarled bushlet.

— *frigidum* is found on the highest Corsican mountains. It appears as a neat tuft of silver stems and leaves and has surprisingly large, white, papery-bracted flower heads.

— *milfordiae* (= *marginatum*) has silver-leaved rosettes growing in flat cushions and beset with short-stemmed crimson buds which expand into large white flowers.

— *selago* resembles a slightly looser, less rigidly upright *H. coralloides*.

— *virgineum* is a handsome plant, probably best in the alpine-house. Its wide silver-haired leaves form loose rosettes and on the 9 in stems are globose buds enveloped in shell-pink papery bracts, which open into large white flowers.

Hepatica [Ranunculaceae]

— *nobilis* (= *triloba*) is a herald of spring. From its tufts of three-lobed leaves spring short stems, each bearing one shapely clear

blue flower. There are several variations on the theme, with white or pink flowers and, although they are now regrettably rarities, with fully double, blue, white or pink flowers.

— *transsilvanica* (= *angulosa*) is rather similar but slightly larger in all its parts, and not so given to producing double or single forms of varying colour.

Hieraceum [Compositae]

Of the many hawkweeds, few are garden-worthy. The following both flower in spring and summer and propagation presents no problems. A reduction rather than an increase in numbers sometimes becomes desirable.

— *aurantiacum* will be allowed space for the sake of its orange-scarlet flowers. A British native, it is sometimes known as 'Grim the Collier'. Because of its ability to spread, take care to place it where it will not become a nuisance.

— *villosum* is very different. It makes shaggy rosettes of leaves, thickly felted with silver hairs and carries its heads of yellow flowers on 1 ft-high stems.

Hippocrepis [Leguminosae]

The common British horse-shoe vetch is *H. comosa*. It is a pretty wildling, but not for the garden. There is a selected form, known as 'E. R. Janes' which is very desirable, making prostrate mats of

1 *Aethionema* 'Warley Ruber'

2 *Alchemilla mollis*

3 *Pulsatilla alpina* ssp. *sulphurea*

4 *Campanula barbata*

5 *Campanula betulifolia*

6 *Campanula herzegovensis* 'Nana'

7 *Campanula poscharskyana*

8 *Catananche caespitosa*

9 *Chamaecyparis obtusa* 'Intermedia'

10 *Tanacetum densum* spp. *amani*

11 *Dianthus haematocalyx*

12 *Dianthus strictus* 'Brachyanthus'

13 *Erinus alpinus*

14 *Edraianthus pumilio*

15 *Euryops acraeus*

16 *Gentiana inverleith*

17 *Gentiana sino-ornate* var. *alba*

18 *Gentiana sino-ornata*

19 *Geranium* 'Ballerina'

20 *Geranium farreri*

21 *Geranium wallichianum* 'Buxton's Blue'

22 *Globularia meridionalis*

23 *Gypsophila repens* 'Letchworth Rose'

24 *Hypericum rhodopaeum*

25 *Inula ensifolia*

26 *Leiophyllum buxifolium*

27 *Leontopodium alpinum*

28 *Leptospermum scoparium* 'Nicholsii Nanum'

29 *Leucogynes leontopodium*

30 *Lewisia* 'George Henley'

31 *Lewisia* 'Pinkie'

32 *Lewisia rediviva*

33 *Lewisia* 'White Seedling'

34 *Linum* 'Gemmell's Hybrid

35 *Lithospermum intermedium*

36 *Maianthemum bifolium*

37 *Neopaxia australasica* 'Montia'

38 *Phlox* 'Chattahoochee'

39 *Rosularia pallida*

40 *Primula marginata*

41 *Ramonda myconi*

42 *Rhodohypoxis baurii*

43 *Saponaria ocymoides* 'Rubra Compacta'

44 *Saxifraga cochlearis* 'Minor'

45 *Saxifraga cotyledon* 'Southside Seedling'

46 *Saxifraga cebenensis*

47 *Saxifraga fortunei* 'Rubrifolia'

48 *Saxifraga longifolia* 'Tumbling Waters'

49 *Sedum humifusum*

50 *Sedum hispanicum* 'Minus'

51 *Sedum oreganum*

52 *Sempervivum arachnoideum*

53 *Sempervivum arachnoideum*

54 *Sempervivum imbricatum*

55 *Sempervivum heuffelii*

56 *Sempervivum marmoreum*

57 *Thymus carnosus*

58 *Trachelium asperuloides*

59 *Thalictrum kiusianum*

60 *Tropaeolum polyphyllum*

61 *Verbascum dumulosum*

62 *Viburnum tomentosum* 'Lanarth'

63 *Viola cornuta alba*

tangled leafy stems smothered in spring and early summer with bright yellow flowers.

Homogyne [Compositae]

This genus is certainly not sensational, but I like to have a few plants of *H. discolor* for the sake of its neat tufts of kidney-shaped, thick-textured leaves which are dark-green above but silvery on the undersides. The reddish-purple tiny flowers are borne in small heads on 3 in stems.

Houstonia [Rubiaceae]

In its native North America, *H. caerulea* is usually called 'bluetts'. It likes a cool or lightly shaded position where it will form loose mats of short stems dressed with tiny, glossy leaves. The myriads of soft blue flowers are carried on 3 in stems in summer.

Hutchinsia [Cruciferae]

Nothing could be better to lighten a darkish, cool corner than a small colony of *H. alpina*, an easy little European alpine. The cushions of small, pinnatifid leaves are concealed in summer beneath clouds of snow-white flowers on 2 in stems. It has a subspecies, *H. a.* ssp. *auerswaldii*, which has darker foliage and slightly larger flowers.

Hypericum [Guttiferae]

This is a valuable race of sun-loving plants, ranging from tiny alpines to tall, bushy shrubs. Some of them hail from warm climates and benefit from the protection afforded by an alpine-house. They ask for no special soils and are propagated by seeds or cuttings and they blossom in the height of summer.

— *balearicum* comes from the Balearic Isles and asks for some winter protection. It grows as a dwarf, rigidly upright shrublet with leathery, evergreen leaves and solitary yellow flowers at the growth tips.

— *cerastioides* (= *rhodopaeum*) may begin to flower as early as May, its large golden flowers being well displayed over the loose mats of entangled stems and hairy leaves. **24**

— *coris* is an erect, 6–9 in bush, with small leaves set in whorls on the stems and yellow flowers in axillary clusters.

— *empetrifolium* comes from Greece and some of the many islands thereabouts and is usually grown in the variety *prostratum* (= *oliganthum*). It is ideally placed at the edge of a stone trough or sink, or where it can spread over a flat stone in the rock garden. The profusions of yellow flowers are dispersed over prostrate mats of tangled woody stems and tiny, narrow green leaves.

— *olympicum* (= *polyphyllum*) is usually seen under its synonym. This is a wholly desirable little shrubby plant, seldom exceeding 6 in in height. The richly golden flowers are borne in terminal cymes and there is an equally desirable form with flowers of citron-yellow.

— *reptans* is one of the best of the alpine kinds. Its completely flat and ground-hugging stems end in large and golden, saucer-shaped flowers. It comes from the Himalayas, and likes gritty, but not hungry, soil and all the sun it can be given.

Iberis [Cruciferae]

Although there are numerous species of *Iberis* in Southern Europe and Western Asia, only the forms of *I. sempervirens* need concern us here, although plant collectors will doubtless want others. *I. sempervirens* itself is surpassed in garden worthiness by the form known as 'Snowflake', whose flat heads of snow-white flowers are carried on 9 in stems. *I. s.* 'Little Gem' is a smaller version of the same. Then there is *I. pygmaea*, which is no more than a very dwarf variant—and highly desirable. *I. tenoreana* (=*jucunda*) is a pleasant plant, its white flowers often prettily flushed with mauve.

Inula [Compositae]

Given moderately austere treatment, *I. acaulis* is a pleasant enough little unimportance. Give it gritty soil and a sunny place and enjoy its tufts of hairy leaves and short-stemmed yellow flowers in summer. *I. ensifolia* is a taller plant, carrying the golden-rayed flowers on 9 in stems. **25**

Iris [Iridaceae]

An enormous and important genus, catering for all garden tastes, its members range from the tall bearded irises of flower borders to miniature alpine kinds and some which are bulbs. There are also irises for bogs and some will even grow in shallow water. I shall describe only those appropriate to the rock garden.

— *chamaeiris* is a very variable species and is often confused with the not dissimilar *I. pumila*. Any of its forms are worth having and one of the best is *I. c.* 'Campbellii', whose large, indigo-blue flowers are seen on very short stems.

— *cristata* is a dainty North American species, arranging its entwinements of slender rhizomes close to the ground. From the tiny tufts of narrow leaves rise short stems, usually carrying two orange and lilac flowers, the falls bearing a conspicuous white crest. This, and the similar but even smaller *I. lacustris*—previously regarded as a form of *I. cristata*—likes a cool position and well drained soil rich in humus.

— *gracillipes* is a plant from Japan with a dainty charm all of its own. It, too, prefers a cool position and, on its branching stems, which can attain a height of 9 in, are flat, soft lilac flowers, each segment with a handsome golden crest. There is an equally desirable form with white flowers, similarly gold-crested.

— *innominata* from North America is another variable plant. Its most beloved form displays golden flowers veined with buff-brown lines, but seedlings, some of which may be hybrids, provide a host of variants, many with flowers of several pastel and 'art' shades. It should be given soil which does not dry out readily and is full of nourishment. I grow it in full sun, but I am told that it will tolerate some shade.

— *pumila* comes from Asia Minor and various parts of Europe. It is seen in gardens in many selected forms and hybrids with flowers of various colours. It seldom exceeds 6 in in height and relishes an open, sunny position and soil rich in lime.

Jankaea [Gesneriaceae]

It is doubtful if any British nursery includes *J. heldreichii* in its catalogue, but it does occasionally creep into circulation and is always eagerly sought after. The only species in its genus, it inhabits limited areas in the mountains of Greece. It can be compared to a *Ramonda* whose leaves are felted with a dense pelt of silver hairs. The bell-shaped flowers are of clear crystalline blue and appear in the spring. It can be grown in the open but is usually given special treatment in the alpine-house. It likes a crevice between small rocks and a humus-rich soil.

Jasione [Campanulaceae]

Easy-going and summer-flowering, *J. jankae* and *J. perennis* are two quite desirable plants for a sunny position. They both carry rounded heads of blue flowers on 9–12 in stems, those of *J. jankae* being of the deepest blue. They are easily raised from the freely produced seeds, or can be divided.

Jeffersonia [Berberidaceae]

The Natural Order to which *J. dubia* belongs is no guide to its appearance, for it is unlike any kind of *Berberis*. From hard, woody roots it emits wiry stems ending in rounded, often lobed, leaves and the equally thin, erect stems carry a single cup-shaped clear blue flower. It is hardy and can be raised from seeds. It comes from Manchurian woodlands and has a preference for a coolish situation.

Kalmiopsis [Ericaceae]

The only species in its genus, *K. leachiana* has one or two local variants. Native to Western North America, it is a dwarf shrub of very great beauty, demanding lime-free soil and a cool situation. It is a comparative newcomer, having been introduced about 1935 and immediately captivated all alpine gardeners who could provide the necessary conditions. Its evergreen, rounded bushes of about 1 ft in height have dark-green leaves of substantial texture and the stems end in racemes of bell-shaped, gloriously pink flowers in the spring. Increase it from seeds or, with care, from cuttings of semi-ripened wood.

Kelseya [Rosaceae]

Once again this is a monotypic genus, *K. uniflora* being the only known species. A native of cliff faces in North America, it deserves, and is always given, a place among the most precious high alpine cushion plants. It will grow outside and is a fine inhabitant for a hole in tufa rock, or it can be tucked into a niche between rocks in a sink or trough garden. However, it is more often given special alpine-house treatment. It forms tight domes of closely packed stems adorned with tiny hairy leaves. The small, white, pink-flushed flowers sit tight onto the cushions in spring and early summer.

Leiophyllum [Ericaceae]

A valuable, dwarf evergreen, *L. buxifolium* is a lime-hating shrub from eastern North America. In nature it can be almost prostrate, or a bush up to 2 ft in height, but the form commonly grown is around 1 ft high. The woody stems carry leathery green leaves and end in clusters of pink flowers during May and June. **26**

Leontopodium [Compositae]

— *alpinum* is the legendary edel-weiss of mountain meadows and is known and liked by anyone who has anything to do with alpine plants. Although of no startling beauty, its tufts of narrow grey leaves and clustered heads of grey-flannel flowers never fail to charm. It will grow anywhere, in any good, well drained soil. **27**

— *haplophylloides* comes from the Himalayas and is not unlike its European cousin in general appearance, but the whole plant is strongly lemon-scented.

Leptospermum [Myrtaceae]

All the *Leptospermum* that we grow are Australasian and some are dubiously hardy. *L. ṣcoparium* 'Nicholsii nanum' is a precious alpine-house shrublet forming small, dense, rounded hummocks adorned in summer with deep red flowers. **28**

Leucanthemum [Compositae]

I would class *L. hosmariense* among the best introductions of recent years, well deserving the Award of Merit given to it in 1958. Its woody stems make rounded domes and bear silver, deeply cut leaves. The white, yellow-eyed large daisy flowers are carried on 9 in stems all summer. It is a sun-lover.

Leucogynes [Compositae]

The only two species in this genus from New Zealand are *L. grandiceps* and *L. leontopodium*. Rather similar in appearance, they are exciting silver-leaved plants for the alpine-house or for a carefully selected position in peat beds or rich scree beds in the open. They grow as tufts of leathery narrow leaves, sheathed in silver hairs. The small yellow flowers are crowded in terminal clusters and are surrounded by white and woolly bracts. **29**

Lewisia [Portulacaceae]

The entire *Lewisia* genus is an all American group of spring- and summer-flowering rock garden and alpine-house plants. There are many species, some of which have become submerged in a number of strains of hybrid origin which, one has to admit, are of greater garden value than their parents. Supposedly lime-haters, nevertheless they will tolerate a considerable degree of alkalinity if the soil is sharply drained and rich in humus.

The purists may like to gather what they can of such species as *L. columbiana*, *L. cotyledon*, *L.*

finchae, *L. heckneri*, *L. howellii*, *L. mariana* or *L. purdyi*, but they have largely surrendered their individuality and played their part in creating the several named hybrid strains. A few have more moral habits and seldom hybridise.

— *brachycalyx* is a deciduous species which emerges in early spring as a neat tuft of fleshy, narrow leaves with a central cluster of short-stemmed white flowers.

— 'George Henley' is a hybrid with short-stemmed sprays of purple-red flowers in profusion and it has the virtue, which most *Lewisia* lack, of flowering continuously from May until autumn. **30**

— *leeana* is another species apparently averse to inter-marriage. Its fleshy, grey-green leaves, circular in section, set off the panicles of pink flowers, usually during high summer.

— 'Pinkie' is a hybrid, very dwarf and short-stemmed, with many narrow-petalled pink flowers. **31**

— *rediviva* has a thick root (said to be edible if the bitter outer skin is removed) from which emerge clustered narrow, fleshy leaves and huge solitary flowers of rose-pink. **32**

— *tweedyi* is the prizewinner of the genus and, as far as I know, has never married with another *Lewisia*. From its lusty root, rise bold clumps of large and fleshy leaves and, on wiry stems, large, wide-petalled blossoms whose flowers are a suffusion of yellow, pink and apricot colours. There is a selected form with flowers of deep rose-red and a rare albino.

— 'White Seedling' is among the more exciting of recent selections carrying snow-white flowers. **33**

All *Lewisia* benefit from a 'drying-off' period after they have flowered and, when grown in the open, like to be planted on a slope or in rocky crevices, such conditions providing the perfect drainage they demand.

Linaria [Scrophulariaceae]
Some of the plants well known as *Linaria* have now been transferred to the genus *Cymbalaria* q.v.

— *alpina* is the delightful, if short-lived, alpine toadflax whose short stems bear whorls of blue-grey, fleshy leaves; the semi-procumbent stems are adorned with orange and violet flowers all through the summer. Sow seeds to ensure a continuity, or allow it to self-seed.

— *tristis* 'Lurida' is a curiously attractive oddity from North Africa, similar in habit to *L. alpina* but with flowers of yellow-grey, veined with purple-red and with two large patches of deep purple on the lip.

Linnaea [Caprifoliaceae]
The only species is *L. borealis*, a delicate and dainty charmer. The ground-hugging stems grow into tangled mats and carry small, rounded leaves from the axils of which, on very short stems, rise twin-flowers of shell-pink. It likes lime-free soil and a cool position. It is European and American in distribution.

Linum [Linaceae]
One somehow expects flaxes to have blue flowers, and, of course, many of them do, but there are some valuable rock garden kinds with blossoms of brilliant yellow. They are all sun-lovers and ask only for any good, well drained soil. Propagate by seeds or cuttings. They are summer-flowering.

— *arboreum* comes from Crete and has woody, 12 in stems, ending in bold clusters of fine golden flowers. It appreciates warmth, as does *L. campanulatum*, another yellow-flowered species from South Europe. *L. capitatum* also belongs to the yellow-flowered group, as does *L. flavum*.

— 'Gemmell's Hybrid' is a particularly precious garden hybrid which was raised in a Scottish nursery forty years ago. Very compact, it grows as a neat dome of fleshy, grey-green leaves concealed at times beneath the large golden flowers. **34**

— *monogynum* is a New Zealander and, like so many plants from the Antipodes, forsakes tradition and carries pure white flowers on erect, slender, leafy 1 ft-high stems.

— *narbonense* inhabits Spain and Portugal and, especially in its finest manifestations, such as 'Six Hills' Variety', 'Peto's Variety' and 'Gentianoides', is truly magnificent, the elegant, tall, arching stems ending in loose clusters of immense, slightly funnel-shaped flowers of the richest imaginable blue.

— *perenne* var. *alpinum* is a smaller version of *L. narbonense*, carrying its softer blue flowers on shorter stems.

Lithospermum [Boraginaceae]

Most of the plants commonly known as *Lithospermum* are now more correctly named *Lithodora*. The few described here are avid sun-lovers and summer-flowering. Propagate by soft-tip cuttings or from the seeds, which are sparingly produced.

— *diffusum* from South Europe is seldom grown, its place in gardens being taken by the old favourite *L.* 'Heavenly Blue' or the more recent *L.* 'Grace Ward'. There is little difference between them, but the flowers of the latter may be slightly larger and it is certainly more robust. Lime-free soil is essential if either plant is to give

of its best. The wide, spreading mats of woody stems disappear for weeks on end beneath a wealth of gentian-blue flowers.

— *oleifolium* from the Pyrenees is a foot-loose wanderer, spreading by means of underground stems and erupting here and there with tufts of rounded, hairy, grey-green leaves. Its short spikes of flowers are often pinkish in bud but expand into flowers of clear light blue.

— *intermedium* and more erectly shrubby species are now included in the genus *Moltkia* q.v.

Lobelia [Campanulaceae]

Only one species really qualifies and that is *L. linnaeoides*, a tiny plant from New Zealand which makes a flat carpet of frail stems and dark-green, very small rounded leaves. Along the creeping stems are many small white and purple flowers. Give it the cool soil it craves, in a not too hot and dry position.

Lotus [Leguminosae]

The bird's-foot trefoil, *L. corniculatus*, is not admissible to a rock garden, but there is a less invasive form, with double yellow flowers, which is a valuable and colourful carpeter.

Lupinus [Leguminosae]

The tall border lupins are not suitable for rock gardens, but a couple of North American charmers might well find a place there—if obtainable, for they are rarities in cultivation but lovely enough to be eagerly sought.

— *lyallii* makes a 4 in pad of filigree silver leaves and offers clusters of bright blue flowers.

— *ornatus* is a Californian and equally sensational. It is slightly taller, again with silvered foliage and short spikes of intensely blue flowers. They deserve a very special place, or alpine-house treatment.

Lychnis [Caryophyllaceae]

This genus is much confused with at least half a dozen others. *L. alpina* 'Rosea' is a neat little plant forming leafy tufts and carrying its rich pink flowers in tiny heads on short stems in the spring. It grows easily in any good soil, in a sunny place, and comes true from seed.

Lysimachia [Primulaceae]

— *japonica* 'Minuta' likes a shady spot with moisture-holding soil and there will make a film of creeping stems beset with tiny green leaves and starred with many small yellow flowers. Never sensational but pleasing in its quiet way, it comes from Japan and benefits from being occasionally lifted, divided and replanted in fresh soil.

— *nummularia* is the British creeping Jenny and really has no place in the garden, but the form with golden leaves is a nice carpeter for a cool place.

Maianthemum [Liliaceae]

Widespread in Europe, *M. bifolium* also lives in the northern counties of the British Isles, always choosing cool, shady places in which to spread its carpets of heart-shaped leaves and to display the elegant little racemes of tiny white flowers. It will run about, so give it plenty of space. **36**

Margyricarpus [Rosaceae]

From the Chilean Andes comes *M. setosus*, a valuable dwarf plant of shrubby habit. Its woody stems form lax, 1 ft-high bushes. It is evergreen, with dark-green, finely cut leaves. The flowers are scarcely visible, but they are followed by fleshy, pure white berries. Any good soil and an exposed position provide all that it needs.

Mazus [Scrophulariaceae]

These are mostly prostrate, creeping plants, natives of Australasia and also Asia.

— *pumilio* offers mats of dark-green leaves on which sit stemless blue and white flowers.

— *radicans* is similarly flat with bronze-green leaves and white flowers with a violet blotch.

— *reptans* is more vigorous and has purple-blue flowers.

Meconopsis [Papaveraceae]

Most of the *Meconopsis*, although lovely, are too tall for the average rock garden, yet they come from alpine environments and cannot really be excluded. One or two of the smaller kinds, such as *M. quintuplinervia*, with its loose tufts of softly hairy leaves and pendant lavender blue flowers, carried singly on 1 ft-high stems, can be used. So can the Welsh poppy, *M. cambrica*, but this is liable to become a nuisance as it seeds all too freely and should really be relegated to the wild garden, where its yellow or orange flowers can be enjoyed in safety. Of the taller kinds, the following are recommended: *M. grandis*, *M. integrifolia*, *M. napaulensis*, *M. paniculata* and *M. superba*.

Mentha [Labiatae]

The majority of the mints should dwell in the herb garden, but pretty little *M. requienii* from Corsican heights is a pleasant little creeper for cool places. It spreads as a mere film of soft green leaves close to the ground and is studded in spring and summer with stemless lavender flowers. It is intensely aromatic.

Mibora [Gramineae]

A tiny, annual alpine grass, *M. minima* is very useful for growing in association with small alpines which like companionship, e.g.

Gentiana verna, which dislikes growing in solitary splendour. It never becomes invasive and appears as neat tufts of thread-fine bright green leaves and seldom grows more than 1 in high.

Micromeria [Labiatae]

These are all dwarf shrubs with woody stems in tangled huddles and small flowers in shades of pink and purple. They are all extremely aromatic and may have to be protected from cats, who find them quite irresistible. Species to seek are *M. corsica*, *M. croatica*, *M. piperella* and *M. rupestris*. They all relish hot, dry positions in any good soil.

Mimulus [Scrophulariacae]

To make these happy it is essential to provide moist conditions, not necessarily bogs, but moisture-retentive soil in not too hot and dry a situation. *M. primuloides*, from North America, makes prostrate carpets of wee, hairy leaves. On 1 in stems it carries single small, but brilliantly yellow flowers. It often dies out if not fairly frequently divided and replanted. Most of the other kinds commonly grown in rock or water gardens are hybrids or clones of *M. cupreus* and are met with under such names as 'Bees Dazzler', 'Fireflame', 'Red Emperor' and 'Whitecroft Scarlet', the last named being especially desirable and neatly dwarf.

Minuartia [Caryophyllaceae]

Many plants previously known as *Arenaria* have now been relegated to this genus.

— *stellata* grows into flat, hard pads of tiny, congested, hard green leaves on which sit stemless white flowers. Give it very gritty soil and a place in full sun.

— *verna* is a rare British native, forming tiny hummocks of emerald leaves over which flutter innumerable small white flowers. It is another good companion for other small alpines.

Mitchella [Rubiaceae]

The tiny evergreen shrublet *M. repens* comes from North America and is for a cool place in lime-free soil. Its trailing stems are set with pairs of glossy green leaves and the small white flowers are quickly followed by red berries.

Moltkia [Boraginaceae]

These sun-loving, summer-flowering plants are often included in the genus *Lithospermum*. They are all dwarf shrubs with woody stems and grey or grey-green leaves and carry their blue flowers in short, often arching cymes. Any of the following are desirable: *M. doerfleri*, *M. froebelii*, *M. intermedia* (35), *M. petraea* and *M. suffruticosa* (= *graminifolia*).

Morisia [Cruciferae]

The only species in this genus, *M. monanthos* (= *hypogaea*), grows in the sea-washed sands of Corsica. In gardens it should be grown in full sun and very sandy soil. The narrow, toothed leaves form compact tufts, centred by clusters of large yellow flowers. It can be increased by root cuttings.

Myosotis [Boraginaceae]

Few of the European forget-me-nots qualify for the rock garden, although some of the named forms of *M. alpestris*, such as 'Ruth Fischer', which has crimped leaves and heads of light blue flowers on 9 in stems, are not out of place in moist soil and a cool position. *M. rupicola*, a rare inhabitant of mountains in the north of the British Isles, is probably only a miniature form of *M. alpestris*, but it is a gem, bearing its brilliant blue flowers on very short stems over tufts of hairy leaves. It should be grown in very gritty soil to ensure that it remains a Lilliputian. From Australasia come some more exciting species, mostly with white or yellow flowers. The one most likely to be found in catalogues is *M. spathulata*; it, and other New Zealanders, are happiest in an alpine-house.

Myrtus [Myrtaceae]

The only myrtle which can find a

place here is *M. nummularia*, a prostrate, creeping shrub from South America. The thin, reddish, woody stems grow into mats of entangled branches, beset with tiny dark green leaves of thick texture. The small white flowers appear in the summer and are followed by pretty pink berries. A good peat garden shrublet, it should be given lime-free soil.

Neopaxia [Portulacaceae]

A fairly recent introduction from the mountains of Australia, *N. australasica* is hardy in a warm and sunny spot. Its prostrate, succulent stems are dressed with blue-grey, rather waxy leaves and the many rounded flowers are white or soft pink and carried on very short stems in summer. 37

Nierembergia [Solanaceae]

A hardy South American, *N. repens* (=*rivularis*) creeps around with underground stems from which erupt small, narrow leaves and large, almost stemless, saucer-shaped white flowers in summer. If planted in rich soil near to a gravel path, it will spread out into the pathway where it appears to be happier.

Oenothera [Onagraceae]

This entirely American genus provides a few good rock garden plants as well as taller kinds to decorate herbaceous borders and flower beds. They are all sun-lovers and grow in any good soil. They can be propagated by seeds or cuttings.

— *acaulis* (=*taraxacifolia*) comes from South America and makes low clumps of dandelion-like leaves centred with groups of almost stemless, large white, or soft yellow flowers.

— *caespitosa* is an exception, deserving a place in an alpine-house. Grow it in large, shallow pans of gritty, humus-rich soil and it will amaze you when it expands its enormous white, fragrant flowers. It is not easy to propagate, but will grow from root cuttings.

— *fremontii* resembles a smaller, refined version of *O. missouriensis*.

— *missouriensis* is a robust and handsome plant. One well established plant will sprawl its lax and leafy stems over a considerable area, but pays a wonderful rent for the space it occupies as it produces a summer-long succession of huge yellow flowers.

Omphalodes [Boraginaceae]

— *cappadocica* comes from the Caucasus and is a common garden plant. A colony in a cool corner will make a brave early spring display when the clear blue flowers appear above the tufts of heart-shaped leaves.

— *luciliae* is a gem to be treasured. It inhabits cliffs in Greece and should be given narrow crevices in which to grow. The trailing stems bear rather waxy, blue-grey leaves and loose racemes of clear blue flowers. It is a confirmed lime-lover and a sun-lover too.

— *verna* is similar in many ways to *O. cappadocica*, but slightly smaller and earlier flowering. It also has a charming albino form with pure white flowers.

Onosma [Boraginaceae]

Not many of the several known species of *Onosma* are grown. They are all lovers of sun and dry conditions and are found in Asia Minor and Central Asia.

— *albo-pilosa* has narrow, roughly hairy leaves in dense tufts and tubular white flowers with a pink flush.

— *taurica* is similar in habit but its blossoms are yellow and very fragrant. Both are valuable wall plants.

Origanum [Labiatae]

These are sun-loving plants for warm positions, mostly from Mediterranean climates. *O. dictamnus* is the Cretan dittany and a very handsome sub-shrub with round, thick leaves felted with white hairs. Its pink, tubular flowers are, as in all the species, displayed amongst showy, colourful bracts. Any of the following are of similar habit and very decorative, with flowers of pink

or purple: *O. hybridum, O. laevigatum, O. pulchellum, O. rotundifolium* and *O. tournefortii. O. vulgare* 'Aureum' is just the golden-leaved form of the common marjoram, but it does make a neat and colourful mound of golden foliage in the rock garden.

Oxalis [Oxalidaceae]

There are literally hundreds of species of *Oxalis* distributed over the temperate and tropical world. The genus contains a few pernicious weeds, almost impossible to eradicate once firmly established, but none of those mentioned below need be feared.

— *acetosella* is the dainty little wild stubwort, or wood sorrel, and is not a garden plant except in its elegant form, 'Rosea', which has rose-pink flowers and is a delightful inhabitant of a cool corner.

— *adenophylla* comes from Chile and, from a curious bulb-like structure of loose scales, throws tufts of crinkly grey leaves, amidst which nestle the large, funnel-shaped white flowers, their petals softly pink-veined.

— *enneaphylla* is from the windy Falkland Islands. It makes long, narrow chains of scaled tubers from which rise the silvery leaves and large, glistening flowers which may be white or soft pink.

— *lobata* has curious habits, which must be known before it can be fully appreciated. From tiny bulbs it emits, in the spring, tufts of emerald-green leaves. In a few weeks these disappear, but be patient, for, in the autumn, up will pop a similar tuft of foliage, this time accompanied by galaxies of short-stemmed golden flowers. It is one of the few plants I know with a double dormant period. It, too, comes from South America and likes gritty, peaty soil.

— *magellanica* creeps about harmlessly, forming mats of tiny, dark green leaves, on which sit pearly white flowers in abundance.

Papaver [Papaveraceae]

There are just a few enchanting tiny poppies which, in spring and summer, add their gay colours to the rock garden. They are seldom long-lived, but seed themselves without becoming nuisances.

— *alpinum* flaunts its solitary flowers, on short stems, over the neat clusters of segmented leaves. The colour ranges from white through shades of pink, and some plants have yellow blossoms.

— *miyabeanum* came to us from Japan. It is a daintiness with rosettes of softly hairy grey leaves, toothed at the margins; the large yellow poppy flowers nod from the top of the short stems. It does not self-sow as readily as *P. alpinum* and it is wise to save a few seeds to ensure a succession.

Paradisea [Liliaceae]

The St Bruno's lily, *P. liliastrum*, of the European Alps is the only species in its genus. There are no difficulties in growing it, given good, well drained soil, an open, sunny position, and the patience to set out young seedlings and wait for the 2 or 3 years necessary for strong, flowering plants to result. From its tufts of very narrow leaves, spring 15–18 in stems bearing loose heads of white, fragrant flowers in high summer. It should be increased from seed.

Paraquilegia [Ranunculaceae]

Acclaimed as the most beautiful of all alpine plants and with some justification, *P. anemonoides* is a great rarity from Kashmir and elsewhere in the Himalayas. It demands, and deserves, very careful cultivation. Wedge it between small pieces of rock in deep pans or pots in the alpine-house; the soil should be gritty but not lacking in humus. The leaves are delicately cut and grey, almost fernlike and, just above the foliage, carried singly on slender stems, are the rounded, rich lavender-blue flowers, each with a central boss of golden stamens. It will grow in acid or alkaline soil, with, possibly, a slight preference for the latter.

Parnassia [Saxifragaceae]

The grass of Parnassus, *P. palus-*

tris, is well worth cultivating in moist soil. Over the small, heart-shaped leaves on wiry stems are several white flowers, the petals veined green.

Parochetus [Leguminosae]

Although it is not completely hardy, *P. communis* is such an attractive carpeter for moist places that is is worthwhile potting a few pieces and keeping them under glass for the winter. On its prostrate, spreading, leafy stems it displays, in late summer and autumn, pea-flowers of gentian-blue.

Paronychia [Caryophyllaceae]

There are several species of these sun-loving, mat-forming, easily grown plants, valuable for their grey or silver foliage and for the silver bracts which enclose their unimportant flowers. Any of the following are desirable: *P. argentea*, *P. capitata* and *P. serpyllifolia*.

Penstemon [Scrophulariaceae]

This important genus of showy, dwarf plants, occurs mostly in North America, with a few in Mexico and one in North-East Asia. Their nomenclature is more than a little confused but, whatever their names, they are valuable and showy plants for open, sunny positions, sheltered where possible from cold east winds, which they dislike, and planted in any good garden soil. I have selected the best and those most likely to be found in nurserymen's catalogues.

— 'Amethyst' is a hybrid, making 1 ft-high bushes, with flowers of tubular shape and rich amethyst colour.

— *confertus* is of almost prostrate habit, carrying on its short stems flowers of cream-white or pale yellow.

— *cristatus* grows in 6-in bushlets and has flowers of rich reddish-purple.

— *davidsonii* consists of dwarf bushes of woody stems with fleshy, grey-green leaves and large flowers of rich pink.

— *heterophyllus* can attain a height of 18 in and, in its best forms, is a fine plant with many flowers of rich gentian-blue.

— *menziesii* is a variable species, usually a low bush of about 6 in tall with flowers of violet-blue. The dwarfest, and possibly the best, form is *P. m.* 'Microphyllus'.

— *pinifolius* has needle-fine leaves on 9 in stems and narrow tubular flowers of bright crimson-red.

— *roezlii* is probably not the plant in cultivation, but the one going under its name is a splendid thing. It forms low bushes and has a wealth of rich rose-red flowers.

— *rupicola* is one of the very best. Quite dwarf, it has thick, grey-green leaves and rose-carmine flowers.

— *scouleri* grows up to 1 ft in height, or a little more, and has narrow, leathery leaves and many clusters of purple flowers. It also has a rather delightful form with pure white flowers.

— 'Weald Beacon' is a hybrid of unknown parentage, raised many years ago in a Surrey garden in the British Isles. It resembles *P. roezlii* (of gardens) in habit, but has flowers of rich purple-red.

Petrocallis [Cruciferae]

In some books and catalogues *P. pyrenaica* may still be found as *Draba pyrenaica*. A cushion plant of the high European Alps and screes, it grows as a neat mound with small, wedge-shaped leaves. In early spring it is decorated with many short-stemmed white flowers which are flushed with lilac and sweetly fragrant. Give it very gritty soil and sun.

Phlox [Polemoniaceae]

With one possible exception, the phloxes are confined to America in their distribution. They vary from the familiar, tall border kinds to tiny cushion plants. They flower mostly during the spring and early summer and, on the whole, are easily grown in open, sunny positions and in any good, well drained soil.

— *adsurgens* is one of the exceptions. It prefers a cool, lightly shaded position and is an excellent peat garden plant. Its prostrate stems spread into tangled mats and the short stems bear several nicely rounded flowers, usually of salmon-pink, although the colour is variable.

— *amoena* has rather untidy mats of tangled stems fostering 9 in stems, each of which carries several pink or purple flowers.

— 'Chattahoochee' is a fairly recent introduction and is probably a natural hybrid. It is a splendid thing, with a liking for soil rich in humus and a not too hot and dry position. On the 1 ft-high leafy stems are elegant heads of rounded, rich violet-blue flowers with a centre of deeper colour. It will sometimes flower itself almost to death and a few cuttings should be rooted periodically to ensure continuity. **38**

— *douglasii* is a cushion plant, now much confused with *P. subulata* with which it has hybridised freely. Any of its named forms are desirable, smothering their humped domes with innumerable flowers which range, according to kind, from pure white to deep pink.

— 'Millstream' is another recently introduced natural hybrid and of great merit. Its good, large, clear pink flowers, each with a ring of white and a central red star are carried on 6 in stems.

— *stolonifera* is seen at its best in the two named clones, 'Blue Ridge' and 'Pink Ridge'. It is of loose habit with the shapely flowers borne on 9 in stems. Both forms are apt to die out after a time and a few divisions or rooted cuttings should be kept in reserve.

— *subulata* represents the most popular race of dwarf phloxes. It would be difficult to identify the type species as it exists as a host of named kinds. All of them make dense hummocks of congested growth which disappear beneath the myriads of almost stemless flowers. Any alpine plant catalogue will provide an abundant choice, with colours ranging from white through all shades of pink, purple and blue to brilliant red.

Phyteuma [Campanulaceae]

The most appealing member of these cousins of *Campanula* is the cliff-dwelling *P. comosum* from European mountains, now renamed *Physoplexis comosa*. The plant is an exciting challenge. Give it a deep, narrow crevice, either outdoors or in the alpine-house, with gritty, humus-rich soil, and be patient. If it approves of what you have provided, it will make tufts of kidney-shaped, rather leathery leaves over which hover the short-stemmed heads of curiously shaped, long-tubed, purple-blue flowers. It is not one of the easiest alpines to grow but its beauty justifies any effort to please it.

Of the several other species, all Europeans, sun-lovers, summer-flowering and easy to grow, *P. hemisphaericum* is the smallest, forming small tufts of grass-fine leaves and rather flattened heads of blue flowers. *P. orbiculare* is taller and offers handsome globular heads of purple-blue blossoms. *P. scheuchzeri* carries its blue flowers in rather flattened heads.

Pinellia [Araceae]

As with *Arisarum proboscideum*, *P. ternata* is a plant to delight the children and amuse their parents. It is a tiny aroid with small tubers, from which spring arrow-shaped leaves and small, hooded flowers, for all the world like the head of a hooded cobra. Its method of self-increase is also amusing, for it forms little snail-like bulbils on the leaf stems, which will detach when mature and can be grown on as individuals.

Pinguicula [Lentibulariaceae]

This is a race of insectivorous plants, some hardy, others tropical. Their rosettes of sticky leaves hold and absorb small insects, thus providing them with the nitrogen which is lacking in their natural boggy environments. *P. alpina* is a rare British native with yellow-throated white flowers. *P. vulgaris*, also British, has violet flowers but the best for garden purposes is *P. grandiflora*, an occasional native of Irish bogs. It has rosettes of wide, fleshy leaves and, on 4–6 in stems, bears large flowers of rich violet-blue. They all die back to a small resting bud during the winter.

Plantago [Plantaginaceae]

If you have spent hours endeavouring to remove *P. major* from your lawns and other places you may think that no plantain should find a place in your garden, but *P. argentea* and *P. nivalis* make amends for their undesirable relation. Both make tufts of narrow leaves felted with a dense pelt of silver hairs. Their flowers have little or no value and they should be regarded as foliage plants for sunny positions.

Pleione [Orchidaceae]

Few alpine-house, or cold greenhouse plants can rival for beauty the exquisite *Pleione*. These near-hardy orchids have surged into popularity during the past two decades and there is now a wide selection from which to choose. Most of those with clonal names are forms of a widely variable species, *P. bulbocodioides*. (Under this umbrella name you will find *P. formosana*, *P. pricei*, *P. limprichtii*, *P.* 'Polar Sun', *P.* 'Oriental Splendour' and many others.) Then there are true species, such as *P. hookeriana*, *P. humilis*, *P. pogonoides*, and *P. yunnanensis*.

They need no special orchid compost and will grow well in a soil with a loam base, fortified by liberal quantities of peat or leaf mould with enough sharp sand or grit added to make it an 'open' mixture. When at rest they like to be kept very dry, but in growth they will endure liberal watering. Frost-free protection is all they ask for and some of them, *P. limprichtii* in particular, can be grown in the open. I know of several colonies flourishing in peat gardens without any form of winter protection.

Their typically orchid flowers are carried on short stems, usually before the aspidistra-like leaves develop, and range in colour, according to kind, from pure white through shades of pink and purple to almost red, with handsome markings on the lips and in the throats of their beautiful flowers. The exception to this colour range is precious *P. forrestii*, a great rarity, whose blossoms are clear yellow, marked with orange and brown.

Polygala [Polygalaceae]

The common British milkwort, *P. vulgaris*, is not a garden plant, but the rare nearly related *P. calcarea* makes a neat tuft of dark green leaves and has lax racemes of clear blue flowers. From European mountains comes little shrubby *P. chamaebuxus*, with woody stems, tiny leathery leaves and axillary clusters of yellow and cream flowers. The form 'Grandiflora' has larger carmine and yellow flowers. Give it peaty soil and light shade or a cool northerly aspect.

Polygonum [Polygonaceae]

Generally speaking, *Polygonum* are more border plants than rock plants. *P. tenuicaule*, a tiny Japanese plant, forms prostrate tufts of small leaves on spreading stems and heralds the spring with white flowers in short racemes. *P. vaccinifolium* adorns the late summer and autumn. Its woody stems grow into trailing mats and the small, leathery leaves take on rich autumn tints. The racemes of heather-pink flowers provide a welcome splash of rich colour. It is a fine wall plant and consistently abundant in its floral display.

Potentilla [Rosaceae]

With a few exceptions, *Potentilla* are easy, sun-loving plants for any good soil. They flower during the summer months and can be propagated by division, cuttings or seeds. The shrubby forms of *P. fruticosa*, though handsome and valuable, are generally too large for the rock garden, but remember them if you have a position for dwarf, long-flowering, easily grown shrubs.

— *alba* is, in my opinion, a neglected plant. It sprawls about, perhaps not too tidily, but its mats of divided leaves, silver-haired beneath, set off the large white, yellow-eyed flowers admirably.

— *aurea* spreads its carpet of green leaves in neat array and adorns them with loose sprays of small, but bright yellow flowers. There is a semi-double form and another, *P. a.* 'Chrysocraspedia', which enriches the colour to orange.

— *crantzii* (= *alpestris*) grows in tufts rather than mats, of palmate, divided leaves and its yellow flowers, carried in small clusters are orange-blotched at the base of the petals.

— *eriocarpa* comes from the Himalayas, unlike the above species, which are all European. It is a prostrate plant with grey-green leaves and has quantities of rounded yellow, short-stemmed flowers throughout the summer.

— *megalantha* comes from Japan and is a beauty. Its large, velvety leaves, palmate and softly hairy, make bold clumps from which rise short, erect stems bearing remarkably large golden flowers.

— *nitida* is one of the exceptions to be noted. It inhabits the high screes of the Alps in Europe where it spreads into wide mats of silver foliage upon which rest the almost stemless rich pink flowers. It needs a little more attention in gardens. Give it very gritty soil and full sun.

It will flower more freely if made to endure a spartan existence.

— *tonguei* is a most worthy hybrid. On its spreading stems are dark green, sometimes bronzed leaves and the apricot flowers are suffused with crimson. It flowers persistently throughout the summer months.

Primula [Primulaceae]

Here is a great family of more than 500 species, distributed worldwide and with widely different requirements. Some are bog plants, others dwell in rocky crevices; others are woodland plants and some live in open alpine meadows. The tall Asiatic candelabra primulas are not really rock garden plants, although they are magnificent by the waterside and in boggy places. I shall omit the exquisite Himalayan *Petiolaris* primroses. Those gardeners living in the humid, cool north may be able to succeed with such delights as *P. aureata*, *P. boothii*, *P. bracteosa*, *P. edgeworthii*, *P. gracilipes*, *P. scapigera*, *P. sonchifolia* and *P. whitei*, but in the south they demand very special care and attention and even then success is not assured. The primulas fall into two groups according to their distribution.

Primulas from Asia

— *capitata* has symmetrical rosettes of neatly arranged toothed leaves, heavily powdered with white farina. On 6–9 in stems are flattened, globular heads of small tube-shaped blue flowers. An especially good form to seek is *P. c.* ssp. *mooreana* which has very richly coloured flowers.

— *chionantha* is impressive, with long, strap-shaped leaves which are farinose when young, but grey-green as they age. The more than 1 ft-high stems carry umbels of white, golden-eyed fragrant flowers.

— *clarkei* comes from the high flowery valleys of Kashmir. It is a tiny plant with tufts of small leaves and rich pink flowers, occurring either singly or in small clusters. It is essential to lift, divide and replant it every 2 or 3 years.

— *denticulata* is the easy and ever popular drumstick primrose. From its dormant roots, it emits strong clumps of robust leaves and 1 ft-high stems carrying the bold, rounded heads of flowers. The colour varies from white to glowing rose-red. If it is desired to maintain one particular clone, it can be increased with ease from root cuttings.

— *forrestii* comes from Yunnan and is exceptional in preferring a dry position. It it seen at its best when planted in the crevices of a sunny wall, or wedged between stones in a large pan or pot in the alpine-house. It has woody rhizomes and vigorous tufts of leathery, dark green leaves. The golden, orange-eyed flowers are borne in rather one-sided umbels.

— *ioessa* is a daintiness from the Himalayas. The toothed leaves lack farina and the 6–9 in stems carry loose heads of funnel-shaped, rather pendant, fragrant flowers. The colour varies from almost white to purple.

— *rosea* is a lover of really moist soil and will even grow when submerged in a few inches of water. It is one of the first plants to flower, displaying its bright rose-red flowers in the earliest days of spring. The first flowers open as they emerge from the soil and the stems gradually increase to about 12 in long.

— *secundiflora* is a good rock garden plant, although it likes a modicum of dampness in the soil. It bears heads of pendant, wine-red flowers on 9 in stems.

— *sikkimensis* resembles the preceding species in all but the colour of its flowers, which are yellow. Both species are fragrant.

— *warszenewskiana* is a very desirable species. It is distributed from the Himalayas to Turkestan and grows as a neat carpet of small, finely toothed leaves. On the short stems are umbels of rose-red, yellow-eyed flowers. It benefits from fairly frequent division and replanting.

— *yargongensis* (= *wardii*) carries, on its 9 in stems, umbels of flowers which vary from pink to purple or mauve and, occasionally, white.

Primulas from Europe, America and the Caucasus

— *allionii* is from a limited area in the Maritime Alps of France and is an alpine-house treasure. It is by nature a cliff-dweller, making close hummocks of softly, hairy, slightly sticky leaves, jewelled in early spring by many almost stemless, large, rose-red flowers. There are several named clones and hybrids; all are beautiful. Given care with watering, especially during the winter, it is not a difficult plant. The soil should be gritty but rich in humus.

— *elatior* is the oxlip, native to Europe, the USSR and the British Isles. Its leaves are like those of the cowslip and the heads of pendant yellow flowers, orange-marked in the throat, make it a very desirable plant for a cool position.

— *farinosa* is known as the bird's-eye primrose. Small tufts of farinose leaves produce short stems on which are heads of pink, yellow-eyed flowers. It is apt to be short-lived, but is easily raised from the plentiful seeds it provides. It does not relish being sun-baked in hot, dry soil.

— *frondosa* from Bulgaria can be likened to an enlarged *P. farinosa* with the farina on the undersides of the leaves and larger heads of pink flowers, usually with a white eye. It likes the same growing conditions as its smaller cousin.

— *hirsuta* is a variable European alpine species forming rosettes of broad leaves, covered with a film of reddish hairs. Seek it in its best form as the flowers vary from dingy purple to clear pink or red.

— *integrifolia* comes from the Pyrenees, and forms a neat cluster of tiny, narrow, stiff leaves. Its reddish-violet flowers appear on very short stems.

— *juliae* is a very old garden plant, introduced from the Caucasus many years ago. It has proved a prolific parent and has fostered, together with the primrose, a race of hybrids which exist, with clonal names, under the umbrella name of *P. × pruhoniciana* (= × *juliana*). The type plant, now rather a rarity in gardens, forms mats of short rhizomes on which are rounded, toothed leaves and bright purple-red flowers on 1 in-high stems.

— *latifolia* (= *viscosa*) is a European alpine, sometimes confused with *P. hirsuta*, but a distinct species. It has broad, lax, slightly sticky leaves and many-flowered umbels of slightly tubular flowers, usually fragrant and purple or dark violet in colour.

— *marginata* glorifies rocky crevices on the cliffs of the Maritime Alps. Infinitely variable in leaf form, it usually has richly farinose foliage with a jagged margin. The flowers vary in colour from soft lavender to rich blue or purple. There exist many named selections, all extremely attractive and easily grown, either in the open or in the alpine-house. **40**

— *minima* is the smallest of the European alpine species, making neat tufts of closely packed rosettes of wedge-shaped leaves toothed at the apex. On very short stems it offers surprisingly large rich pink flowers. Give it gritty scree soil and a sunny position.

— *parryi* is North American, has narrow leaves and, on 1 ft-high stems, carries umbels of tubular, purple, yellow-eyed flowers. It prefers lime-free soil and a cool position.

— *pubescens* must be regarded as an umbrella name covering a host of hybrids and selections, many with individual names. They are all easily grown, dwarf and decorative.

— *scotica* is a tiny aristocrat from the far north of the British Isles. Over its wee rosettes of farinose leaves it carries, on very short stems, heads of small, rounded violet-purple flowers with white or yellow throats. It is short-lived but very lovely. Save and sow a few seeds each year.

— *suffrutescens* is an unusual, almost shrubby primula from California. Happier in an alpine-house than out-of-doors, it makes low, spreading bushes of thick stems dressed with narrow, leathery leaves. Amidst the terminal leaves are short stems carrying fragrant, pink, yellow-eyed flowers. Give it lime-free, gritty soil. It can be easily increased from cuttings.

— *veris* is the common cowslip, too well known to need description.

— *vulgaris* is the common primrose. It has one notable geographic form, *P. v.* ssp. *sibthorpii*, with clear pink flowers, which was recently awarded a First Class Certificate by the Royal Horticultural Society — an unusual honour for any form of primrose.

Hybrid primulas of the European group

There exist a great many natural hybrids between the European species of *Primula*, all extremely desirable and easily grown. Any of the undermentioned would be welcome additions to a garden: *P.* × *berninae, P.* × *bileckii, P.* × *deschmannii, P.* × *fachinii, P.* × *forsteri, P.* × *goeblii, P.* × *heeri, P.* × *huteri, P.* × *juribella, P.* × *kellereri, P.* 'Marven', *P.* × *salisburgensis, P.* × *steinii, P.* × *venusta* and *P.* × *vochinensis*.

Pterocephalus [Dipsaceae]

An easy sun-lover, *P. parnassii* from Greece makes mats of grey, hairy leaves over which hover heads of purple-pink flowers.

Ptilotrichum [Cruciferae]

A useful, sun-loving dwarf and shrubby in habit, *P. spinosum* (= *Alyssum spinosum*) covers its rounded bushes of twiggy, spiky stems with myriads of white flowers. There is a desirable form whose flowers are soft pink.

Pulsatilla [Ranunculaceae]

The pasque flower and several other plants previously included in the genus *Anemone* have now been transferred to this genus.

— *alpina* is a glory of alpine meadows in Europe with ferny foliage and very large pure white flowers on tall stems. The blossoms are followed by handsome heads of long-awned seeds. *P. a. apiifolia* (= *sulphurea*) has clear yellow flowers and prefers lime-free soil.

— *vulgaris* is the beloved pasque flower, of which numerous forms are cultivated.

— *vernalis* is one of most beautiful European alpines. Over low tufts of finely dissected leaves it produces, on short stems coated with golden-bronze hairs, upturned goblets, opal white and iridescent within, with a bold tassel of golden stamens. The outer side of the flowers shimmer in a haze of silky gold and violet hairs.

Ramonda [Gesneriaceae]

This interesting and valuable genus contains just three species:

R. myconi from the Pyrenees and *R. nathaliae* and *R. serbica* from the Balkans. There is a strong family resemblance between them; they all make flat rosettes of wide, roughly hairy leaves and produce, on short stems, single, wide, flat, rounded flowers of purple-blue. They are spring-flowering and like to grow in chinks between rocks or the stone of a cool wall. They may be propagated by seeds or, carefully, by leaf cuttings. *R. myconi* in particular may produce forms with white or pink flowers amongst its seedlings. These must, of course, be propagated vegetatively. **41**

Ranunculus [Ranunculaceae]
Both British buttercups, *R. acris* and *R. bulbosus*, have handsome double-flowered forms which are good garden plants, although rather tall for most rock gardens. Their type forms, of course, would never willingly be admitted to any garden.
— *alpestris* is a delightful pygmy from the Alps of Europe with small, heart-shaped and lobed leaves and circular pure white flowers on very short stems.
— *amplexicaulis* comes from the Pyrenees and has entire, slender leaves which clasp the stem and large pure white flowers on 9 in stems. Amongst its seedlings, occasional forms appear which are semi-double.

— *calandrinioides* comes from the Atlas Mountains of North Africa. From a stout, deeply delving root it produces long, wide, grey-green leaves and 12 in stems carrying very large, cup-shaped white flowers, often flushed with soft pink. Although hardy, it flowers so early in the year—January/February—that the flowers are often damaged and it is then happier in an alpine-house. Propagate by seed.
— *crenatus* is another little European from the high Alps with snow-white flowers on very short stems.
— *ficaria* is the common British lesser celandine and a lovely weed, not admissible in gardens. It has, however, several well behaved variations. Perhaps the best of these is *R. f.* 'Aurantiaca', whose flowers are a rich coppery-orange colour. Then there are white forms, primrose-yellow forms and some attractive ones with fully double yellow flowers. The giant of the race is *R. f.* 'Major' which displays its large golden flowers on robust 1 ft-high stems—but it is rather invasive and should be kept for wild corners where it can spread at will.
— *glacialis* should be appreciated as it deserves in the high Alps—and left there, for it is very difficult, indeed, almost impossible, to please in cultivation. Experts are still struggling to persuade it to

adapt to garden conditions. Its enormous flowers of dazzling whiteness are carried on short, branching stems above the grey-green, fleshy, deeply cleft leaves and, as the flowers age, they change to pink and rose-red. If you can get a specimen, try it in almost pure grit, kept sopping wet in the spring, and keep it in the alpine-house.

— *gouanii* is a Pyrenean with tufts of large, lobed and rounded leaves and enormous golden buttercups.

— *gramineus* is from alpine meadows and has narrow, grassy leaves and 9 in stems carrying saucer-shaped yellow flowers in profusion.

— *montanus* is seen at its best in the garden-raised cultivar 'Molten Gold'. It is neat, dwarf and very free-flowering with many golden blossoms on 4 in stems.

— *parnassifolius* is a beauty when at its best, but there are poor forms to be avoided. Over little clumps of thick, heart-shaped dark green leaves are large, many-petalled flowers of immaculate whiteness. It loves a very gritty scree soil.

Raoulia [Compositae]

Most of the members of this genus come from New Zealand.

— *australis* is the best known, makes a mere film of silvered, tiny leaves and is good ground cover

for tiny alpine bulbs. It can suffer in a severe winter but will recover quickly if top-dressed with gritty soil in the spring.

— *glabra* is different and easy, making green mats, studded with clusters of wee cream-white flowers.

— *lutescens* is a mere smear of minute rosettes on the soil and becomes golden in the early summer with innumerable little clusters of yellow flowerlets.

Rhodohypoxis [Hypoxidaceae]

The hearts of all gardeners have been won by *R. baurii*. It comes from the Drakensburg Mountains of South Africa but is surprisingly hardy. From tiny bulbils issue clusters of small, narrow, hairy leaves and, from May until the autumn, an endless succession of flowers. It is infinitely variable and the colour of the blossoms may be white or pink, on to a glowing red. Several forms have been selected and given clonal names. It likes a warm, sunny place in soil which does not dry out. At no time is it more than 1 or 2 in high. **42**

Rhodothamnus [Ericaceae]

A rare and precious dwarf shrub, *R. chamaecistus* comes from limestone areas of Europe. It makes a neat, hummocky evergreen bush and the woody stems end in clusters of pink flowers. It is slow-growing and likes plenty of humus in its soil mixture.

Rosularia [Crassulaceae]

A neat little plant, *R. pallida* has rosettes like those of a hairy-leaved *Sempervivum*. The yellow, tubular flowers are borne in short erect spikes in early summer. It is an avid sun-lover suitable for any good soil. **39**

Rubus [Rosaceae]

Few of this genus are rock garden plants, but *R. arcticus* is a prostrate, creeping plant, emitting from its running underground stems tufts of small trifoliate leaves and quite large pink flowers. It likes peaty soil and a shaded or cool situation.

Sagina [Caryophyllaceae]

There are weedy plants in the genus, but one or two are of value. This applies especially to *S. boydii*, a rarity discovered once only, many years ago, on a Scottish mountain. It is best in an alpine-house, or a sink or trough garden, where it will make a tight dome of congested, tiny, very glossy green leaves. The flowers are valueless, but it is an admirable cushion plant. *S. glabra* (= *Arenaria caespitosa*) is a commoner, but useful. It spreads into wide mats, especially in its 'Aurea' form, of thin golden shoots starred with small white flowers. A good rock garden ground coverer.

Salix [Salicaceae]

The really dwarf willows are splendid little rock garden shrubs. There is a host of them from which to choose. They all carry attractive catkins. Detailed descriptions of the following are not really necessary but all are to be recommended : *S. apoda* (always ask for the male form) *S.* × *boydii, S. herbacea, S. lanata, S. myrsinites, S. myrtilloides, S. repens* (the British native species; dwarfest forms should be sought) *S. reticulata, S. serpyllifolia* and *S. uva-ursi.*

Sanguinaria [Papaveraceae]

The Canadian bloodroot, *S. canadensis*, is a plant for a cool position in peaty soil. From its thick, red-sapped roots rise, in the spring, folded grey leaves which expand to reveal a pearly bud which opens into a pure white flower. The life of the blossoms is brief, but the even more beautiful double-flowered form will last for a day or two.

Saponaria [Caryophyllaceae]

An easy European plant, *S. ocymoides* is ideal for crevices in walls. It hangs down in a curtain of leafy stems which disappear in early summer beneath sheets of pink flowers. There is a flat-growing, compact form named 'Rubra Compacta' which is neat enough for a sink garden and is especially richly coloured. 43

Saxifraga [Saxifragaceae]
From this vast and important genus of more than 300 known species and countless hybrids, clones and selections, I shall choose largely species, mentioning only a few of the best hybrids. Unless otherwise stated all are sun-lovers asking for open, gritty compost.
— *aizoides* comes from Europe and the British Isles, and is found in moist places. Its tuffets of short stems are clothed in fleshy, narrow leaves and the terminal clusters of flowers are yellow, spotted on the petals with orange-red.
— *aizoon* is now more correctly called *S. paniculata*. It is an infinitely variable plant, scattered in its various forms throughout the Alps. Two deserve special mention : *S. a.* 'Lutea' and *S. a.* 'Rosea', one with flowers of soft yellow and the other of pink. Both are pretty exceptions in a group of mostly white-flowered plants.
— × *apiculata* is a garden hybrid of long-standing excellence. Over its cushions of tiny green, hard leaves it spangles an abundance of soft yellow flowers in compact heads. There is also a variant with white flowers. A similar hybrid,

named 'Boston Spa', has flowers of rich yellow.
— *burseriana* is very early-flowering and is also a variable species. Its grey, hard, tiny leaves are gathered into tight hummocks and the short stems carry large white flowers. Forms of special merit to seek are 'Crenata', 'Gloria' and 'His Majesty' and there is another, probably a hybrid, *S. b.* 'Lutea', with yellow blossoms.
— *caesia* is a high alpine cushion plant forming scabs of congested wee grey rosettes and carrying its white flowers on 3 in stems.
— *callosa* (= *lingulata*) exists in several distinct geographical forms. The rosettes are composed of narrow, silver-grey leaves and the white flowers are borne in arching panicles.
— *cebenensis* makes hard domes of compressed, sticky and hairy leaves. On 2 in stems it displays surprisingly large white flowers. It is at its best in an alpine-house. 46
— *cochlearis* is a silver saxifrage with compressed hummocks of crowded rosettes and dainty foxtail plumes of white flowers on 6–9 in stems. It has minor and major forms offering some variation on the same theme. 44
— *cotyledon* is another variable species with a wide distribution, extending throughout Europe into Scandinavia and even into North America. Its wide, leathery leaves

make handsome rosettes, from which rise fairly tall stems carrying innumerable white flowers, which are, in some forms, heavily speckled with pink or red. It is a splendid crevice or wall plant. **45**

— *diapensioides* is even smaller and more congested than *S. caesia* and also has white flowers on very short stems.

— 'Elizabethae' is a hybrid similar to *S. × apiculata* but with flowers of richer yellow.

— 'Esther' is a pretty hybrid between *S. aizoon* 'Lutea' and *S. cochlearis*. It has pads of grey-green leaves and heads of creamy-yellow flowers on 6 in stems.

— *fortunei* is an Asian species and invaluable for late summer-flowering. It likes a cool position out of direct sunlight. The large, lobed and rounded leaves are green above and often bronze on the underside (*S. f.* 'Rubrifolia' has entirely bronze-red leaves) and the erect, branching, 1 ft-high stems carry flights of white flowers which have one or two of the lower petals much longer than the remainder. **47**

— *granulata* is the wild meadow saxifrage, but in its double form it is an excellent plant. From roots which have round nodules it emits tufts of crenate leaves and white flowers in elegant 9 in sprays.

— *grisebachii* comes from Greece and is usually grown in the form known as 'Wisley Variety', which is an improvement on the type. It has lovely symmetrical rosettes of silvered leaves. The centre of each rosette elongates in the spring to become a crozier of crimson bracts between which nestle the small flowers. It is best regarded as an alpine-house plant.

— × *irvingii* and 'Jenkinsiae' are companion plants. Both are hybrids and rather similar. They form flat pads of tightly congested tiny grey-green leaves with almost stemless soft pink flowers in early spring.

— × *kellereri* is a hybrid and one of the first saxifrages to flower. Over its grey rosettes it carries on short stems several tubular pink flowers.

— *lilacina* from the Himalayas grows as a flat pad of closely packed rosettes, with the tiny leaves arranged in a quadrangular pattern and stemless soft lilac flowers. Give it gritty, lime-free soil and light shade.

— *longifolia* is the magnificent cliff saxifrage of the Pyrenees, seen in its most splendid form as 'Tumbling Waters'. The large rosettes of symmetrically arranged narrow grey leaves are handsome enough in themselves but become superb when carrying the long, arching sprays of innumerable white flowers. It is monocarpic, the rosette which flowers dies. It does sometimes make side-rosettes which can be rooted as cuttings. **48**

— *oppositifolia* is a rare British native but has a wide European distribution. Very early flowering, it decorates its prostrate carpets of dark green, tiny leaves with large purple-red flowers.

— *retusa* is a small and refined version of the *S. oppositifolia* group, except that the small rich red flowers are carried in short erect corymbs.

— × *urbium* is the universally popular plant well known as *S. umbrosa*, or London pride. It is of hybrid origin, but there are some miniature forms of it worth noting, in particular the 6 in daintiness known variously as 'Walter Ingwersen' and 'Clarence Elliott'. Two great plantsmen discovered the plant almost simultaneously and it crept into commerce under both names. Each swore that his was the dwarfest and best! There is also a form of *S.* × *urbium* with nicely variegated foliage.

— *valdensis* makes hard tufts of silver rosettes. It looks very much like a congested form of *S. cochlearis* and is sometimes confused with that species.

Another group of invaluable saxifrages is known as the 'mossies'. These are cushion-forming, with soft foliage and a liking for positions that, whilst exposed to sunlight, are not hot and arid. There are a great many of them, all hybrids, clones and selections and any good alpine plant catalogue will offer a wide choice, but a few of the best to seek are 'Carnival' (crimson-rose), 'Diana' (pale pink), 'Dubarry' (crimson), 'Elf' (a miniature with carmine flowers), 'Four Winds' (deep crimson), 'Gaiety' (rich pink), 'James Bremner' (very large white flowers), 'Mrs Piper' (red), 'Pompadour' (dusky crimson), 'Sanguinea Superba' (crimson) and 'Winston Churchill' (large clear pink flowers).

Scutellaria [Labiatae]

Flowers of true, deep blue are uncommon enough to make *S. scordifolia* a very desirable plant. A native of Korea, it spreads by underground roots to form small colonies from which spring erect 9 in stems which carry many narrowly tubular deep blue blossoms in summer.

Sedum [Crassulaceae]

This is another immense genus from which only a selection can be described. With one or two exceptions, all sedums are sun-lovers and most flourish in even the poorest of soil.

— *acre* is one of the weeds of the group, which many a gardener regrets having planted, although it is pretty.

— *album* is widely distributed in Europe, Asia and North Africa. In gardens it can be a weed but has value as a ground-cover in sunny places. It has better-behaved forms, such as *micranthum*, *murale*, and 'Coral Carpet', which are neat and non-invasive and have colourful leaves.

— *anacampseros* is amusing and decorative. Its sprawling, brown, snake-like stems have blue-grey leaves and end in heads of pink flowers.

— *caeruleum* is one of the few annuals which I willingly would admit to the rock garden. It inhabits a few Mediterranean islands and makes low, rather bushy plants, shrouded in summer with clouds of misty-blue flowers. It will seed itself harmlessly.

— *cauticola* from Japan is invaluable for late summer and autumn colour. It is ideally planted in a crevice, from which it can hang its thin, woody stems, clothed in blue-grey leaves and ending in large heads of crimson flowers.

— *hispanicum* itself is very short-lived, but the form 'Minus' is a good perennial, growing as a flat carpet of blue-grey tiny leaves with white, pink-flushed flowers on 1 in-high stems. **50**

— *humifusum* comes from Mexico and is happier in an alpine-house, in moisture-holding soil. The mossy, compact pads of tiny leaves, tinted red in winter are studded with quite large yellow flowers. **49**

— *kamtschaticum* from North Asia covers its mats of dark green leaves with bright yellow flowers. There is also a rather handsome form with richly variegated foliage.

— *lydium* is particularly neat, forming rounded cushions of crowded stems and small leaves which adopt bronze tints in summer. The short stems carry close-packed heads of white flowers.

— *oreganum* is native to North America and pleases with its pads of flat, fleshy bronze-red leaves and flat cymes of bright yellow flowers. **51**

— *palmeri* comes from Mexico and should be kept in the alpine-house. Its 1 ft-high stems branch freely and have glaucous, fleshy leaves, ending in pendant heads of yellow flowers. It flowers spasmodically throughout the summer.

— *pilosum* is a biennial and dies after flowering. It has grey, hairy leaves arranged in *Sempervivum*-like rosettes and, on short, branching stems, shows waxy rose-red flowers. It, too, is happier under cover but can be used in trough and sink gardens.

— *primuloides* comes from Yunnan and is a mat of dark green fleshy leaves over which are large, white, bell-shaped flowers adorned with dark stamens.

— *pulchellum* represents another departure from the family rules and relishes a boggy situation. The reddish, prostrate stems have narrow green leaves and the rose-red flowers are displayed in starfish-shaped heads during mid to late summer.

— *sempervivoides* is another biennial with rosettes like those of a hard-leaved *Sempervivum*. When it flowers, the centre of the rosette rises into a neat pagoda headed by a cluster of scarlet flowers.

— *spathulifolium* is North American and a universal favourite. The type is less often grown than 'Purpureum', whose round, fleshy leaves are purple and dusted with white farina. Also desirable is 'Cappa Blanca', which is so heavily farinose that it appears to be white-leaved. Both have branching heads of golden flowers on short stems.

Selaginella [Selaginellaceae]
A delicately beautiful soft green club-moss, *S. helvetica* makes splendid ground cover in cool shady places. In winter the foliage often changes to rust-red shades.

Semiaquilegia [Ranunculaceae]
A dainty cousin of the aquilegias, *S. adoxioides* comes from China. From elegant tufts of typically 'aquilegia' foliage rise 1 ft-high stems carrying loose heads of purple-brown spurless flowers.

Sempervivella [Crassulaceae]
Of this small Himalayan genus, only one is commonly grown, *S. alba*, a pretty little *Sempervivum*-like rosette of green, pink-flushed and fleshy leaves and short sprays of sizeable white flowers in early summer.

Sempervivum [Crassulaceae]
Although these succulent plants will submit to very austere growing conditions, they will also repay rather more generous treatment. They do not need very rich soil, but they are as appreciative of nourishment as any plant. They do need all the sunlight they can get and must have good drainage. They will endure drought with equanimity and will be happy enough in only a shallow layer of soil. Although a large group, it does not contain a great many species. The majority of those grown and listed in catalogues are hybrids and geographical or selected forms of named clones. I will describe a few of especial merit, which are sufficiently distinct to deserve mention.

— *allionii* (= *Jovibarba allionii*) is an attractive species with very globose rosettes of yellowish, incurved leaves. The flowers are yellow but are not produced with any generosity.

— *arachnoideum* is the cobweb houseleek which furnishes its neat rosettes of green and pink leaves with a fine network of white hairs. It is seen at its finest in the form *S. a.* (= *laggeri*). The flowers are rose-red. **52, 53**

— × *calcaratum* is probably a hybrid. Its provenance is uncertain although it is reasonable to suppose that one parent was *S. tectorum*. It makes magnificent large rosettes of green and purple leaves.

— *ciliosum* forms dense clusters of globose rosettes of incurved grey-green leaves, felted with fine white hairs, which are especially conspicuous in the form *S. c.* var. *borisii*. The flowers are yellow.

— *grandiflorum* has the dubious merit of being unmistakably identifiable by the smell of goats emitted by its leaves when roughly handled. The slightly one-sided rosettes are handsome, the leaves felted with sticky hairs. The flowers are yellow, each petal purple-spotted.

— *heuffelii* (= *Jovibarba heuffelii*) is a variable and handsome species which does not make its 'babies' on short stolons but increases by division of the rosette. In all its geographical variants it has very hard leaves in dense mounds, the leaves often richly coloured. The flowers are usually yellow, but white forms are known. **55**

— *imbricatum* is a name of dubious authenticity, but it is a handsome plant, shy-flowering and decorative in its rosette formation and colouring. **54**

— *marmoreum* comes from the Balkans and is infinitely variable, but desirable in all its forms, the finest of which is undoubtedly 'Ornatum', whose leaves are rich, glowing red with green tips. **56**

— *tectorum* is the common house-leek, still to be seen growing on roofs. It was illustrated by Dioscorides in his *Materia Medica*, written in the sixth century A.D. It, too, has many forms.

Serratula [Compositae]
In some catalogues, *S. seoanei* will be found as *S. shawii*. It comes from the warmer parts of Europe and is a neat little bush of dark, deeply cut foliage with thistle-like heads of pink flowers in late summer and autumn.

Shortia [Diapensaceae]
Shortias are plants for the peat bed, or lime-free soil in cool and shady places. They are all evergreen.

— *galacifolia* has glossy, rounded leaves in low tufts and each short stem carries one funnel-shaped white flower whose petals flush pink as they mature.

— *uniflora* is Japanese and the glory of the race. Its running mats of woody stems carry glossy, round leaves of thick texture and the flowers are large, soft, clear pink and the petals are delicately fringed.

Silene [Caryophyllaceae]
— *acaulis* is a typical alpine cushion plant, which is found

139

throughout the Northern Hemisphere. Its pads of congested tiny green leaves are freely studded in nature with stemless pink flowers. In gardens it is inclined to blossom less freely.

— *alpestris* comes from limestone regions of Eastern Europe. It is an easy and pretty little plant with narrow, glossy leaves and short-stemmed galaxies of white flowers with fringed petals. There is a form with fully double flowers.

— *hookeri* is from North America and is a treasure for the alpine-house. Its spreading stems have narrow, hairy leaves from the axils of which spring large, soft pink flowers. Give it gritty, but lime-free soil.

— *maritima* is the sea campion of British shores. The type plant has no garden value, but the form with fully double, large white flowers is a splendid wall plant, hanging down in grey-leaved cushions smothered with handsome blossoms.

— *schafta* is by no means an aristocrat but its rose-magenta flowers are carried in abundance on short stems from mid summer until October.

Sisyrinchium [Iridaceae]
This genus of sun-loving, grassy-leaved plants comes from North and South America.

— *angustifolium*, *bellum* and *bermudianum* all have blue flowers and can seed themselves to the point of becoming nuisances, pretty though they are.

— *californicum* and *convolutum* have bright yellow flowers and are no threat to garden space.

— *douglasii* is very different. It dies down in the winter. In early spring it erupts into a cluster of very narrow leaves and, on 9 in stems, bears pendant wine-red bells. There is also a form with pure white flowers.

Soldanella [Primulaceae]
These delightful plants from the Alps are amongst the most enticing of spring-flowering rock garden and alpine-house plants. They do ask for a little more care than might be given to the general run of alpines, but, offer them a cool position in humus-rich but gritty soil and they present no great problem. The claim that they are shy-flowering is possibly because their flower buds, which are developed in the autumn, rest concealed beneath the rounded, evergreen leaves until the spring and they all too often fall prey to slugs. They all have circular, leathery green leaves and carry their exquisite pendant, bell-shaped flowers daintily on short stems. The family colour is blue or purple, but albinos are known. For the best of them seek *S. alpina*, *S. carpatica*, *S. minima*, *S. montana*, *S. pindicola* and *S. villosa*,

the last named being the easiest of them all to please.

Tanacetum [Compositae]
These are aromatic plants which include the common tansy.

—*densum* ssp. *amani*, formerly *Chrysanthemum haradjani*, is a tufted plant with dissected silver foliage and large white daisy-like flowers. **10**

— *herderi*, is a neat and decorative silver-leaved bush, less than 1 ft in height which carries heads of yellow flowers. It relishes all the sun it can get in a hot and dry position.

Tanakaea [Saxifragaceae]
The only species in its genus, Japanese *T. radicans*, is a plant for the peat bed or a cool and shady place in lime-free soil. On woody stems it bears evergreen, leathery, heart-shaped leaves, toothed on the margins. In late spring it offers short cymes of small white flowers.

Thalictrum [Ranunculaceae]
Consisting mostly of tall, border plants, this genus does include a few dainty miniatures.

— *kiusianum* is one of the best of these. It comes from Japan and, on its short, wiry stems carries pretty leaves and loose and elegant sprays of small but numerous purple flowers. **59**

— *orientale* is very precious. It is slow-growing and dwarf and, over its *Adiantum*-like foliage show erect 6–9 in stems carrying large, clear pink flowers. It is happiest in an alpine-house, but is hardy enough to set in a sink or trough garden.

Thlaspi [Cruciferae]
A European high alpine, *T. rotundifolium* is loved by every rock gardener. It inhabits the shingles and screes and, from a deep tap root, spreads by underground stems from which erupt tufts of thick, fleshy smooth leaves. In early spring it produces flat heads of fragrant rose-red flowers.

Thymus [Labiatae]
Useful, sun-loving, mostly aromatic plants, the thymes vary from low bushes to creeping kinds.
— *carnosus* comes from sunny Portugal and is an erect 12 in bush with small, rather fleshy leaves and heads of white flowers. **57**
— *cilicicus* is a comparatively recent introduction from Anatolia. It is not completely hardy but is beautiful enough to justify a position in an alpine-house. On mats of soft, green, slightly aromatic foliage, it develops large clusters of vividly lilac-pink flowers.
— *citriodorus* is commonly known as lemon-scented thyme and has several excellent forms. 'Silver Queen' is variegated green and white and 'Aureus' is golden. All

forms grow as neat, low bushes and are strongly aromatic.

— 'Doone Valley' is a hybrid of uncertain parentage. Its mats of dark green leaves are freckled with golden variegation. Crimson buds open into lavender flowers in small, rounded heads.

— *herba-barona* comes from Corsica and is of no special floral value, but the whole plant, stems and leaves, is strongly carraway-scented.

— *lanuginosus* forms a flat carpet of grey, hairy leaves smothered in spring and early summer with heads of pink flowers. Like *T. serpyllum*, it is a good ground-coverer.

— *membranaceus* comes from Spain and is one of the most powerfully aromatic of all thymes. It forms tidy domes of dark green tiny leaves on woody stems and the small pink flowers are surrounded by quite spectacular white, papery bracts. It needs a really hot, dry position.

— *serpyllum* exists in many named forms, all invaluable as carpeters, both for foliage effect and flower. There are forms with white flowers and others range from pink to deep red. It makes fine ground-cover for small alpine bulbs and is delightful planted in a mixture of varieties.

Tiarella [Saxifragaceae]
From North America comes *T.*
cordifolia, a charmer for a cool spot in light shade and any good soil. The softly hairy leaves adopt beautiful bronze tints and the myriads of small cream-white flowers are carried in fluffy spires. It blossoms in spring and early summer.

Trachelium [Campanulaceae]
One of the most exquisite alpine plants, *T. asperuloides* (= *Diosphaera*) is found wild on the cliffs rising from the River Styx in Greece. The frail thin stems are clothed in wee, soft green leaves and grow into low mounds smothered in the spring beneath massed small powder-blue flowers. Surround it with small rocks and give it very gritty but humus-rich soil. It asks for, and deserves, alpine-house conditions. **58**

Trientalis [Primulaceae]
A frail and dainty plant, *T. europaea* likes cool peaty soil in shade. Its thin rhizomes wander harmlessly underground and from them spring short stems with a whorl of small leaves at the top from which rise short stems bearing starry white flowers.

Trollius [Ranunculaceae]
Mostly tall bog plants, there are two miniatures for moist soil in the rock garden. *T. pumilus* and *T. yunnanensis*, both Asiatics, grow only to a height of about 6 in and

display rounded, brilliantly yellow flowers.

Tropaeolum [Tropaeolaceae]
For a superb plant to set at the top of a wall, or where it can hang down over a large rock, choose *T. polyphyllum*. From its large tubers develop asparagus-like shoots which lengthen into 3 ft trails of silver leaves and golden flowers. Plant it deeply in any good, fertile soil and in a sunny position. **60**

Tunica [Caryophyllaceae]
Pretty little *T. saxifraga* is not an aristocrat, but an easy, dainty, summer-flowering, sun-loving plant, it bears sheets of small pink flowers on 6 in stems. There are two variations, one with double pink flowers and one which is double and white.

Uvularia [Liliaceae]
The shade-loving *U. grandiflora* (=*sessiliflora*) native to North America is for lime-free soil. From its rhizomatous roots rise glossy green leaves and the 9 in stems carry pendant, tubular bells in spring and early summer.

Vancouveria [Berberidaceae]
Of the three species in this North American genus, only one is commonly grown. *V. hexandra* resembles the epimediums, to which it is nearly related. From the tufts of soft green leaves on wiry stems

rise panicles of small white flowers. It likes shade and peaty soil.

Verbascum [Scrophulariaceae]
There are three excellent dwarf, shrubby verbascums for the rock garden or alpine-house, all relishing a warm sunny position.
— *dumulosum* has rigid, 1 ft-high woody stems with grey, softly hairy leaves. Each branchlet ends in a raceme of clear yellow, purple-eyed flowers. **61**
— *spinosum* comes from Crete and is even more spiky and spiny, with grey, toothed leaves and yellow flowers.
— 'Letitia' is a hybrid between the two. It occurred as a chance seedling in the Wisley Gardens of the Royal Horticultural Society, growing between the parents. It is intermediate in appearance between the two and it blossoms over a long summer period.

Veronica [Scrophulariaceae]
Many veronicas have been re-assigned to the genera *Hebe* and *Parahebe*, which are all shrubby, mostly New Zealand plants. Of those that remain, several are good rock garden plants, with a few aristocrats for the alpine-house. They are spring- and summer-flowering.
— *armena* sends up, from a woody root, erect, 9–12 in leafy stems,

terminating in loose heads of bright blue flowers.

— *bombycina* is a gem from the Lebanon and likes warmth. Grow it in the alpine-house or in a nook of a sink or trough garden. It likes gritty soil. Use the watering can with discretion. On its mats of prostrate stems, clothed in grey leaves, it discloses china-blue flowers.

— *filiformis* is to be recommended only if there is ample space over which it can spread. It will also seed far and wide. Remember that it is a weed, but a pretty one, for its prostrate mats of leaves become studded with myriads of soft blue flowers.

— *pectinata* has trailing stems clothed in grey, softly hairy leaves. The type plant has blue flowers but the form more often seen has pink blossoms. It is very attractive and a good, non-invasive ground coverer.

— *perfoliata* is not an alpine, but I like and appreciate its oddity and undeniable beauty. It comes from Australia, but is quite hardy. On long, arching stems it has wide, blue-grey, stem-clasping leaves and short racemes of violet-blue flowers, the petals veined with darker colour. It looks like anything but a conventional *Veronica*.

— *prostrata* exists in gardens as a group of clonally named forms, all easy, useful, free-flowering, low-growing plants. According to the particular clone the flowers may be white, pink or some shade of blue. Some of the best are 'Spode Blue', 'Royal Blue', 'Alba', 'Mrs Holt' (pink), 'Nana' (very dwarf) and 'Kapitan' (blue).

— *telephifolia* is another aristocrat, from Asia Minor, and should be given especial treatment in the alpine-house. The creeping stems bear small, waxy silver leaves and there are short-stemmed bright blue flowers in generous sheets. Again, give very gritty soil and take care with the watering can.

Viburnum [Caprifoliaceae]

These handsome medium-sized shrubs of dense spreading habit, although not alpines, provide a splendid background for a rockery. *V. tomentosum*, the Japanese snowball, is most attractive with its creamy-white flowers surrounded by white-rayed florets. **62**

Viola [Violaceae]

Here, in a universally popular family are the violets, violas, violettas and pansies.

— *aetolica* comes from Eastern Europe and is a small neatness with tufts of toothed leaves and clear yellow flowers on very short stems; occasionally, the upper petals are marked in violet.

— *biflora* is the little alpine pansy that peeps brightly at you from beneath and between the rocks where it habitually shelters. It spreads across Europe into Northern Asia and even into North America. On the prostrate stems are small, kidney-shaped leaves and clear yellow flowers, usually in pairs on the very short stems. It dislikes being sun-baked.

— *calcarata* is one of the universal European alpine violas. The creeping rhizomes produce lance-shaped leaves and, on 4–6 in stems, are flowers of rich violet colour. From the more eastern Alps comes the delightful sub-species, *V. c.* ssp. *zoysii*, which has dark foliage and clear yellow flowers.

— *cazorlensis* is one of a trinity of rare, almost shrubby, crevice-haunting violas. It comes from Spain. *V. delphinantha* and *V. kosaninii* can be found in Greece and Albania. They are seldom in cultivation but, if obtained, should be grown in crevices between rocks and given alpine-house treatment. The wiry stems have tiny, hard, narrow leaves and the long-spurred flowers are pink.

— *cenisia* is an alpine from the high screes and can be troublesome. Try it in shallow pans of almost pure grit, with some leaf soil or peat added, where it should ramble about, emitting from its underground stems, tiny tufts of small, rounded leaves and large pink to pinky-purple flowers.

— *cornuta* is frequent in the Pyre-nees and spreads, less generously, through the Alps. The flowers are richly purple, and there is one excellent form with pure white flowers, *V. c. alba*, which is a splendid garden plant, flowering continuously throughout the summer and coming true from seed. **63**

— *cucullata* is frequently confused in gardens with *V. septentrionalis*. Either will like a cool, lightly shaded position and carry large flowers of white, usually veined with purple lines.

— *elatior* is of unusual habit in that it has erect, leafy stems up to 1 ft in height and many typically violet-shaped flowers of soft lavender colour.

— *flettii* is confined to the Olympic Mountains of the State of Washington, USA. Its scalloped leaves grow in neat tufts and the flowers are reddish-violet, veined with darker colour.

— *gracilis* is very dubiously in cultivation, alas, its place having been taken by a number of hybrids and forms which are handsome enough, but lack the aristocracy of the true species. From its low clumps of toothed leaves rise short stems bearing blossoms of rich violet-blue. It comes from Greece and ought to be re-introduced.

— *labradorica* is North American and is at its best in the form 'Pur-purea', whose dark purple, heart-shaped leaves set off so admirably the rich violet flowers. It likes a not too hot and dry position.

— *lutea* is a widely distributed European occasionally found wild in Britain, in northern limestone areas. The neat flowers may be pure yellow, or range through forms with some violet and some white petals.

— *pedata* is another North American, with palmate, deeply cloven leaves and large flowers with the upper petals deep violet and the lower ones paler in colour. Give it a cool position.

— *yakusimana* is Japanese and can claim to be the smallest of all the violas. Its frail, creeping stems are dressed with very small, round leaves, forming mats on which, almost stemlessly, rest the wee, but exquisite, white, purple-veined flowers. It is really too small for the rock garden but is ideal in a trough or sink garden.

Wahlenbergia [Campanulaceae]

— *hederacea* is a frail British species and always grows in moist soil. It creeps about with slender stems carrying tiny, ivy-shaped leaves and axillary flowers of delicious soft blue.

— *serpyllifolia* is becoming distressingly rare, particularly the form known as 'Major'. Selected many years ago for its very large, Tyrian-purple bells, it has been vegetatively propagated for so many generations that it has lost its vigour and is seldom seen at its glorious best. A mat-forming plant, with dark green foliage, its great flowers are borne singly on short stems.

Waldsteinia [Rosaceae]

An easy and invaluable carpeter, *W. ternata* (= *trifolia*) has horizontally spreading, leafy stems and showers of saucer-shaped golden flowers throughout the summer.

Weldenia [Commelinaceae]

A rarity from one or two mountain tops in Mexico and Guatemala, *W. candida* asks for, and deserves, alpine-house conditions. From fleshy, deeply delving roots come great tufts of broad, pointed, leathery leaves, centred by a long succession of cup-shaped flowers of absolutely dazzling whiteness. The Guatemalan form can be recognised by the tufts of white hairs on the surface of the leaves. It likes dry conditions during dormancy and a deep pot or pan in which to plunge its fleshy roots.

Zauschneria [Onagraceae]

The Californian fuchsia, *Z. californica*, should be provided with a hot, dry situation where it will make tangles of woody, grey-leaved stems, adorned in late summer and autumn with showers of tubular scarlet flowers.

Plants for Special Purposes and Positions

Some plants named in the following lists have not been described, but all should be available from nurseries and garden centres carrying stocks of alpine plants. The lists are intended only to indicate plants suited to certain conditions.

Hot and dry places in full sun

Acaena
Achillea
Aethionema
Alyssum
Anacyclus depressus
Andryala aghardii
Anthemis
Armeria
Artemisia
Aster alpinus
Aubrieta
Cistus
Dianthus
Diascia cordata
Dryas octopetala
Euryops acraeus

Genista
Helianthemum
Helichrysum
Hypericum
Penstemon
Phlox 'Cushion' kinds
Potentilla
Pulsatilla vulgaris (= Anemone)
Raoulia
Saxifraga Nearly all kinds
Sedum Except *humifusum* and *pulchellum*
Sempervivum
Thymus
Veronica
Zauschneria californica

Cool and/or shady places

Ajuga
Andromeda
Anemone apennina, blanda, nemorosa
Asarina procumbens
Asperula odorata
Astilbe Dwarf alpine kinds
Calceolaria

Cassiope
Chiastophyllum oppositifolium
Cortusa matthiolii
Cyclamen
Dicentra
Dodecatheon
Epimedium
Erythronium

147

Gentiana asclepiadea
Haberlea rhodopensis
Helleborus
Hepatica
Houstonia caerulea
Lamium
Maianthemum bifolium
Melittis melissophyllum
Mimulus
Mitchella repens

Omphalodes   Except *luciliae*
Parochetus communis
Phyllodoce
Ramonda myconi
Saxifraga fortunei and all × *urbium* forms
Sedum humifusum and *pulchellum*
Soldanella
Uvularia

Crevices in paving
Acaena
Achillea   Dwarf kinds
Antennaria dioica   And forms
Armeria maritima   And forms
Campanula cochlearifolia
Festuca viridis
Mentha requienii

Raoulia
Sagina glabra 'Aurea'
Saxifraga   Especially forms of *S. aizoon*
Thymus serpyllum   All forms
Veronica filiformis

Stone sink and trough gardens
Aethionema 'Warley Rose' and 'Warley Ruber'
Anacyclus depressus
Androsace
Armeria caespitosa (= *juniperifolia*)
Campanula   Dwarf kinds
Crassula sedifolia
Dianthus   Dwarf, cushion-forming kinds
Dryas octopetala
Edraianthus pumilio
Erinus alpinus
Erodium reichardii   And its forms
Gentiana verna 'Angulosa'
Geranium subcaulescens

Gypsophila   Forms of *G. repens* to fall over the edges
Helichrysum milfordiae
Lychnis alpina 'Rosea'
Mentha requienii
Morisia monanthos
Phlox   Cushion-forming kinds
Primula   Dwarf European species and hybrids
Raoulia australis
Salix   Really dwarf kinds
Scleranthus biflorus
Saxifraga   Compact kinds
Sedum   'Cushiony' kinds
Sempervivum
Soldanella

148

Reliable dwarf conifers

Chamaecyparis obtusa   All
  forms; named forms of *pisifera*
  and *plumosa*
Cryptomeria japonica 'Pygmaea'

Juniperus communis 'Compressa'
Microcachrys tetragona
Picea abies   'Bun'-forming kinds

Alpine-house

Anacyclus depressus
Androsace   Especially the
  cushion-forming Aretian
  group, e.g. *A. helvetica,
  vandellii, pyrenaica* and
  pubescens
Andryala aghardii
Arabis bryoides 'Olympica'
Arenaria tetraquetra
Artemisia schmidtii 'Nana'
Asperula suberosa
Campanula formaneckiana
Crassula sarcocaulis
Dionysia
Erigeron aureus

Erinacea anthyllis
Gypsophila aretioides
Helichrysum coralloides
Lewisia
Omphalodes luciliae
Pleione
Primula   European alpine kinds
  and some rarer Asiatic species
Sagina boydii
Saxifraga   Especially very
  early-flowerers
Sedum humifusum
Soldanella
Thymus membranaceus

Further Information

Addresses

Alpine Garden Society, Lye End Link, St John's, Woking, Surrey, GU21 1SW, UK.

American Rock Garden Society, 15 Fairmead Road, Darien, CT 06820, USA.

Edinburgh Royal Botanic Garden, Inverleith Row, Edinburgh 3, Scotland.

Royal Horticultural Society, Vincent Square, London SW1P 2PE, UK.

Scottish Rock Garden Club, 21 Merchiston Park, Edinburgh EH10 4PW, Scotland.

Bibliography

Bacon, Lionel, *Alpines*, David & Charles, 1973.

Clay, Sampson, *The Present Day Rock Garden*, I.C. and E.C. Jack Ltd, 1937.

Farrer, Reginald, *The English Rock Garden*, 1918, 1925.

Huxley, Anthony, *Mountain Flowers in Colour*, Blandford Press, Poole, 1967.

Ingwersen, Will, *Manual of Alpine Plants*, Ingwersen Ltd, 1979, Cassell, London 1991.

Polunin, Oleg, *Flowers of Europe*, Oxford University Press, Oxford, 1969.

Polunin, Oleg and Huxley, A, *Flowers of the Mediterranean*, Chatto and Windus, London, 1965.

Royal Horticultural Society, *Dictionary of Gardening*, Oxford University Press, Oxford, 1951. (A new edition is in preparation for 1992.)

Index of Latin Names

*The figures in **bold** refer to colour plates. Other figures refer to text pages.*